WADSWORTH PHILOSOPHERS SERIES

ON

KANT

Garrett Thomson
College of Wooster

 **Wadsworth**
Thomson Learning™

Australia • Canada • Denmark • Japan • Mexico • New Zealand • Philippines
Puerto Rico • Singapore • Spain • United Kingdom • United States

Printed in the United States of America
1 2 3 4 5 6 7 03 02 01 00 99

For permission to use material from this text, contact us:
Web: www.thomsonrights.com
Fax: 1-800-730-2215
Phone: 1-800-730-2214

For more information, contact:
Wadsworth/Thomson Learning
10 Davis Drive
Belmont, CA 94002-3098
USA
www.wadsworth.com

ISBN: 0-534-57591-9

CONTENTS

Introduction

Kant is one of the greatest philosophers of all time. Few would disagree. But some do. For instance, Franz Brentano (1838-1917) wrote: "I consider Kant's entire philosophy a confusion, and one which gave rise to even greater mistakes." Why this strong condemnation? Perhaps there is something to it. This negative appreciation of Kant reminds us not to take great names for granted. It throws down a challenge: we must show why Kant's theories are philosophically important and insightful.

Kant, a philosopher with a profound knowledge of science, tries to show us why the natural world has the general features it does: why it consists of objects in space and time and causes and effects. In so doing, Kant tries to save scientific knowledge from scepticism and show why metaphysics must fail. This is the project of the first Critique.

Kant was also a philosopher with a deep understanding of morality. He saw that morality not only requires, but is based on, the supreme value of human freedom. We have free-will and for this reason we must respect each other and ourselves as persons. Explaining and justifying this vision of morality is the program of the second Critique.

The first Critique tells us that we live in a mechanical spatio-temporal world. The second Critique tells us that we are free, moral beings. How can the two be reconciled? This is part of the grand question of the whole modern period: how can physics be reconciled with morality and religion?

Many readers have taken Kant to answer these questions by asserting the existence of two worlds: the natural world of things in space and time, and a supersensible realm, beyond space-time and its

1

mechanical requirements. This, as we shall see, is a misunderstanding of Kant's philosophy. Hence the discontent of philosophers such as Brentano.

There is another way to read Kant that does not require the two worlds theory. Kant's own reconciliation of the first and second Critiques, or of science and morality, takes place in the third Critique. There Kant gives us an unusual answer based on natural beauty. Perhaps this does not require a two world theory.

This is why our journey through Kant's philosophy is divided into three parts: the first concentrating on the first Critique and his work on science (Chs. 1-7); the second on his moral philosophy (his work on religion and politics being a part of this (Chs 8-10)). The third part is focused on the reconciliation of the third Critique (Ch.11). In this way, we can bring order and unity to this brief study of Kant's critical philosophy as a whole, and also reply to critics such as Brentano.

I would like to dedicate this book with love to my wife, Helena.

This book owes a lot to many other books written on Kant. I would like to thank Drs. Adrian Moore, Philip Turetzky and Dan Kolak.

The keys to the references to Kant's original texts are given in the bibliography. For instance, for *Critique of Judgment*, the translation used is Meredith's and the reference would be given in the following form: M., p.12. The only exception is the *Critique of Pure Reason*, for which references refer to the original page numbers (e.g. A234).

1

Transcending the Tradition

In 1770 Jacob Lenz writes of Kant's "simplicity of thought and naturalness of life." Herder also praises Kant for the freedom and joyfulness of his soul. Kant's lectures were "discourse at its most entertaining." According to Herder, "merriment wit and humor were at his command." This is not the impression we have of Kant from the *Critique of Pure Reason*. Kant himself writes in his diary: "The method of my discourse...appears scholastic and hence pettifogging and arid."

To comprehend this disparity, we must understand the background to the first Critique. Kant's early life was marked by relative poverty. He lived in boarding houses and never had a home of his own until he was 59. After his doctorate in 1755, he began lecturing as a Privatdozen, receiving only the fees students chose to pay him. He held this position for 15 years. Kant had to be a clear and entertaining lecturer, and indeed he was popular. In 1770 he was appointed to the professorship in Logic and Metaphysics. This was the turning point in his life. His new found position gave him the time and stability to plan an ambitious new work, which became the first Critique.

Kant's early philosophy a variant of a Rationalism typical of the time, fashioned after Wolf and Leibniz. Some time around 1770, after reading Hume, Kant awoke from his dogmatic slumbers and entered an extraordinary process of idea incubation. Kant went through a period of intense reflection for over ten years before publishing. His work is the expression of a long struggle to escape from the presuppositions of the age. This task was made more difficult because written German was still a new language, which had not established a technical vocabulary.

So Kant invented new German words, which are hard to master.

Amazingly, Kant conceived his philosophy as a whole from the outset. In 1771 he was planning a project on the limits of sense and reason which was to cover metaphysics, morals and aesthetics. In 1772, he hoped the first volume on metaphysics would be ready in 3 months. As he worked through the details of his wide ranging ideas, he became aware of the time and effort necessary to plan "a whole new conceptual science." In 1776 he writes of being blocked by a dam. Later he explained that, although the first Critique was "the result of reflection which occupied me for at least twelve years, I brought it to completion in the greatest haste within four or five months, giving the closest attention to contents but with little thought of the exposition . . .." However, he says he does not regret this decision because otherwise, "the work would probably have never been completed at all."

Finally, when the dam broke, a huge torrent came pouring out. The first edition of the *Critique of Pure Reason* was published in 1781, when Kant was already 57. He entered into a period of frenzied writing, articulating the implications of his theory for ethics, politics, history, religion, science, and art. He wrote 8 major books between 1781 and 1797, as well as numerous essays and articles. Each book is regarded as a classic in its own field. They include: *The Critique of Pure Reason* (edition A) (1781) *Prolegomena To Any Future Metaphysics* (1783) *The Groundwork for the Metaphysics of Morals* (1785) *The Metaphysical Foundations of Natural Science* (1786) *The Critique of Pure Reason* (edition B) (1787) *The Critique of Practical Reason* (1788) *The Critique of Judgment* (1790) *Religion Within the Bounds of Reason Alone* (1793) *The Metaphysics of Morals* (1797).

The portal into this startlingly vast domain of thought is the first major book, the *Critique of Pure Reason* which Kant rewrote in part for the 1787 edition, because his readers had great difficulties in understanding his ideas. Before we pass through into this first chamber, we need to understand the surrounding landscape. The brilliance of Kant's philosophy is how it identifies and transcends the two dominant traditions in the philosophy of his time, Rationalism and Empiricism, represented primarily by Leibniz and Hume. `Rationalism' and `Empiricism' are generalizations applied to major philosophers of the 17th and 18th centuries but misleading: philosophers of the time did not regard themselves in these terms. However, it is a useful classification to help understand Kant, even at the risk of being simplistic.

Rationalists believe the fundamental nature of things can be discovered by reason. According to the Principle of Sufficient Reason, everything must have a sufficient cause and in this sense: the universe behaves rationally according to principles grasped by reason. The window breaks. Given an adequate description of the causes, we see the window had to break. Given the causes, it was necessary that it had to happen in that way. Because of this, explanation will amount to logical demonstration. Effectively, this means all truths are necessary truths, and it is in principle possible to know them through reason alone, without recourse to sense–experience. In any case, sense–experience is an inferior form of intellectual apprehension, according to the Rationalists, which does not give us knowledge of the causes of things.

Empiricism of this period consists in two major principles. First, that all knowledge and concepts must be derived from sense experience. Second, that all we directly perceive are our own ideas. Together these principles have dramatically sceptical implications. Given them, how can we know things beyond our ideas, like material objects? How can we even have the concept of such things? Hume saw that given the Empiricist principles, many of our deeply held beliefs cannot be justified. Neither reason nor sense experience can justify beliefs in objects, causation and the self. The two Empiricist principles also imply that there is no a priori knowledge of the world. According to Hume, all necessary truths are tautologies; they are analytic claims which merely reveal the logical relations between concepts and give no substantial knowledge about matters of fact. In this way, Empiricism denies that knowledge of the world can be gained from reason.

Modern Philosophy was in a deadlock. Remarkably, this overall diagnosis of the period is due largely to Kant. He believes that Rationalism and Empiricism share certain fundamental assumptions, which need to be rejected to break the deadlock.

The Questions of the First Critique

As the title of the *Critique of Pure Reason* suggests, Kant's main aim is to critique reason. This means curbing reason's ambition to gain metaphysical knowledge of the world which transcends any possible experience. The Rationalists claimed that such knowledge was possible through reasoning. For instance, Leibniz and Spinoza give detailed theories about the nature of the universe based a view principles supposedly derived from reason. Kant argues that such metaphysical knowledge of the world is impossible. He rejects Rationalism.

Kant has a brilliant strategy. In the early parts of the First Critique, he gives a positive theory of knowledge and experience, which allows him to later criticize Rationalistic metaphysics. This positive theory constitutes a penetrating argument against Empiricism. In other words, Kant criticizes Rationalism by giving a non-Empiricist theory of experience. Accordingly, we can divide the Critique into two parts. In the first, Kant elaborates his non-Empiricist theory of experience (in the Aesthetic and Analytic). In the second part, the Dialectic, he shows how that theory undermines Rationalist metaphysics.

In the first part of the Critique, Kant introduces the key notion of synthetic a priori truths. Kant thinks that there are necessary truths about the world. These are claims which are necessarily true, but which give us information about how things are. Consider the judgment 'the world is spatial.' This does not seem to be merely an empirical truth, because objects must exist in space and the world has to be spatial. In which case, it is an a priori claim. On the other hand, it is a claim which gives us information about the world. It is not true simply by virtue of the meanings of the terms involved. In which case, it is not an analytic truth. We appear to have a claim which is a necessary truth, but which is not analytic. Kant would claim that this is a synthetic a priori truth.

Here there are two pairs of distinctions. On the one hand, analytic-synthetic, and on the other, a priori-empirical. A priori truths are necessarily true; an empirical truth is one which is not necessarily true; an analytic truth is one which is true solely in virtue of the meaning of the terms; synthetic truths are true also by virtue of the way the world is. Examples of analytic a priori truths are: 'all brothers are male', 'a triangle has three sides' 'all effects have a cause.' Examples of synthetic empirical truths are: 'some brothers annoy their sisters', 'John's room has a triangular shape', 'the cause of the explosion is unknown.'

Most assume that all a priori truths are analytic and all synthetic claims are empirical (indeed this is an important tenet of Empiricist philosophy). This assumption rules out the possibility of there being a priori truths about the world. According to this assumption, all a priori truths just give us information about the meaning or definition of terms. Kant rejects that assumption. According to him, some necessary truths are not analytic. Examples are: 'every event has a cause' and 'the angles of a triangle add up to 180 degrees.' Synthetic a priori truths are an essential part of the sciences and mathematics. Geometry consists of synthetic a priori truths about space. Despite their abundance and importance, synthetic a priori truths are puzzling: how is it possible that there are judgments which are necessarily true, but not in virtue of the meanings of the terms involved? Synthetic a priori truths seem like a strange type of proposition. We can understand why there are analytic a priori truths. They are true by definition, or by virtue of linguistic meaning. But how are synthetic a priori truths possible? Kant will answer this question in the first half of the Critique, by developing a new theory of experience and knowledge.

The question sounds technical and this disguises its importance. Two points rectify this impression. First, according to Kant, these synthetic a priori claims form the back-bone of mathematics and science. Therefore, the technical question is equivalent to asking how the sciences and mathematics are possible. If we understand how they work, we can judge whether metaphysics is possible. In other words, by replying to the question `How are synthetic a priori truths possible, Kant will answer the question `How are science and mathematics possible?' which will enable him to answer `Is metaphysics possible?' Second, in answering the question `How are synthetic a priori truths possible?', Kant will develop a sustained argument against Empiricism. Indeed, the question itself already confronts Empiricism, because Empiricist philosophers will claim that all meaningful sentences are either empirical or analytic. They will not admit the possibility of the synthetic a priori. This is a confrontation we must return to later.

The Answer

How are synthetic a priori truths possible? Kant's answer is a non-Empiricist theory of knowledge, the foundation of his criticism of Rationalism. His answer consists in two parts; both are necessary but neither is sufficient. These two central pillars of the Critique are:

1) The necessary conditions of any possible experience:

Kant will argue that space, time and the categories are necessary conditions for any possible experience. All experience must conform to those conditions. Kant tries to establish these necessary conditions with arguments which are called transcendental arguments, the most important of which is the Transcendental Deduction. These arguments try to establish the structural features of experience, those which any experience must have. In Kant's terminology, these are the a priori forms of any possible experience.

2) Transcendental Idealism:

However, establishing that all experience has a necessary structure by itself will not explain how synthetic a priori truths about the world are possible. Additionally we need this: the world must have the same structure as experience. This is exactly what Kant argues. He claims that the world has a certain a priori form (or necessary structure) just

7

because experience must have it. In this manner, the structure of the world depends on that of experience, rather than the other way around.

That should sound odd. Normally, we would suppose that our experience should conform to the world. However, with regard to a priori form or structure, Kant affirms the contrary. Experience dictates to the world. How is that possible? Kant compares this revolutionary idea to that of Copernicus, who gave up the assumption that the Earth is still and the Sun revolves around it. Kant's own Copernican revolution involves giving up the assumption that the world is as it is absolutely in itself. In Kant's language, it involves giving up the assumption that the world of objects in space and time are noumena or things as they are in themselves. Instead we should affirm that objects in space and time are phenomena. This thesis is called Transcendental Idealism.

Transcendental Idealism claims the world of objects in space and time is not absolute but relative to the necessary conditions of experience. By negation, this suggests the idea of the world as it is beyond those conditions or limitations: the world as it is in itself, as noumena. According to Kant, the concept of noumena can have no positive role in theoretical knowledge. It is an empty concept which merely reminds us of the limitations of knowledge and sense - namely the parameters prescribed by the necessary conditions of experience. Transcendental Realism is the doctrine which treats objects as noumena. How does Kant justify his Transcendental Idealism? He is certain that we have synthetic a priori knowledge of the world, because geometry is a clear example of it. Kant was also convinced that neither Rationalism nor Empiricism could explain such knowledge. His own answer is to articulate the necessary conditions of any possible experience. Doing so can at most give us a priori claims about experience. Showing the necessary conditions of experience on its own could not ensure that the real world conformed to those conditions. Therefore, Transcendental Idealism must be true. There is no way to guarantee that the world does conform to the conditions of experience, except by giving up the assumption of Transcendental Realism.

The two pillars explain how synthetic a priori truths are possible, and thereby explain how the sciences and mathematics work. Consider this argument, which encapsulates a vital part of the Critique simply:

1. Sentence S states a necessary condition of experience;
2. The world must conform to the necessary conditions of experience;
3. Therefore, sentence S is a priori true of the world

For 'S' we could put any synthetic a priori claim, such as 'all events are caused.' Premise one is a statement articulating a necessary condition of experience. This is the first pillar. Premise two is a statement of Transcendental Idealism, the second pillar. Together, they imply and explain 3. Obviously, the two premises need detailed support. One of the main jobs of the first half of the Critique is to do that.

An example. According to Kant, 'every event has a cause' is synthetic a priori. It is a necessary truth which is not analytic. How is such a strange truth possible? The first pillar: Kant argues that the category 'cause' is a necessary condition of experience; an uncaused event could not be experienced. The second pillar: as a consequence of Transcendental Idealism, an event which could not possibly be experienced could not be a part of the empirical world. Therefore, every event must be caused. The two concepts 'event' and 'cause' are distinct but linked through the notion of the necessary conditions of experience.

Kant's explanation of synthetic a priori truths constitutes a sustained argument against Empiricism. In essence, his arguments amount to the claim that it does not take into account the necessary structural features of experience. Thus his argument against Empiricism focuses on the first of the two pillars. His argument against Rationalism focuses on the second, Transcendental Idealism.

Two Aspects of Experience

According to Kant, experience requires both a sensory input and a conceptual element. In his language, it requires both intuitions and concepts (or sensibility and understanding). These two aspects of experience are radically different from each other, and one is not reducible to the other. These central Kantian claims supersede the Rationalist and Empiricist traditions. The two traditions treat the difference between sensation and concepts as one of degree, rather than one of kind. For example, Empiricists, Locke and Hume regard concepts as faint copies of sensory impressions. Rationalists, Leibniz and Spinoza think of perception as lower grade and confused form of thought. Rationalists assume that in principle knowledge can be known by reasoning, while the Empiricists assume that all knowledge must be derived from sense experience. Both assume in their own way that there is only one source of knowledge.

By distinguishing intuitions and concepts, Kant transcends both traditions. He argues that sensible intuition and the concepts of the understanding are both necessary for experience and knowledge.

Moreover, for him, the difference between them is one of kind. He says: the senses can think nothing and the understanding cannot receive intuitions. Intuitions are the sensory element within experience, which is passively received and which makes our experience of particulars. Concepts are the classificatory or general element within experience. Since the one does not make sense without other, we should not think of them as elements of experience which can exist independently. This why I call them aspects of experience. Neither the sensory nor the understanding alone suffice for experience: 'intuitions without concepts are blind; concepts without intuitions are empty'. This is how Kant's theory transcends both Empiricism and Rationalism. Against Empiricism, he claims that intuitions without concepts are blind. This means that sense-data or sense impressions without concepts are non-descript. They could not constitute an experience. Against Rationalism, he claims that concepts without intuitions are empty. Apart from their role in experience, concepts have no real sense.

A Map

All experience must have a certain order or a priori form. Kant's investigation into these a priori forms divides into two parts, reflecting the distinction between sensible intuitions and concepts. Both the faculties of sensibility and the understanding have a priori forms. In the Aesthetic, Kant investigates the a priori forms of sensibility, which are space and time. In the Analytic, he investigates the a priori forms of the understanding, which are the categories. This defines the format of the positive side of the Critique. Kant then attacks dogmatic metaphysics in the Dialectic. This constitutes the critique of the faculty, Reason.

Part of the Critique	A priori Form	Faculty
Aesthetic	Space and Time	Sensibility
Analytic	Categories	Understanding
Dialectic	---	Reason

The major divisions of the book reflect that there are three major faculties. Sensibility and Understanding which are both necessary for experience (and are investigated in the Aesthetic and Analytic) and, Reason, which is not necessary for experience. This is why, strictly speaking, Reason does not have an a priori form. As we shall see, the Ideas of Reason are not necessary conditions of experience.

10

2

The Necessary Conditions of Experience

The first pillar of the Critique is the necessary conditions of experience (the second is Transcendental Idealism, which is the theme of the next chapter). Kant argues for two kinds of necessary conditions: space and time, which are the a priori forms of sensibility, and the twelve categories, which are the a priori forms of the understanding. The heart of the Critique consists in Kant's attempt to argue that the categories are necessary conditions of experience. This consists in what are called the Metaphysical and Transcendental Deductions.

Before diving into the details, let us see why Kant's approach is new. First, Empiricists regard concepts as faint copies of sensory images, which is implicit in their claim that all ideas are derived from sense experience. Kant rejects this. He regards concepts as rules for making judgments, which means that they are not like copies of inner pictures. This enables Kant to show that there is a difference in kind between the sensory and conceptual aspects of experience.

Second, Empiricists tend to reify concepts or to treat them as things or items in the mind. Kant avoids this. He regards the meaning of concepts in terms of the function they have in judgment. Third, Empiricists ignore the structural features of experience and knowledge, the focus of Kant's concern.

11

The Metaphysical Deduction

In the Metaphysical Deduction Kant tries to list the candidates for the title of categories. Later, in the Transcendental Deduction, Kant tries to show that the categories are indeed necessary conditions for experience. Obtaining the list of candidates must be done according to a principle. Kant sets this out as an argument.

1) First, he establishes that judgment must have a form. When we make the judgment `the coal is black', the concepts `coal' and `black' form the content of the judgment; they direct what the judgment is about. The verb `is' is not part of the content of the judgment. It determines the form or the logical structure of the judgment. In this way, it is fundamentally different from those other concepts. Kant lists the forms of judgment, which he obtains from Aristotle.

2) Second, Kant argues that perceiving is a kind of judging. To see a table is to make judgments about it. In claiming this, Kant is advancing a view of perception which is fundamentally different from that of the Empiricists, who assumed that perception consists solely in the passive reception of sense-data or impressions.

These two steps enable Kant to argue that sense experience should have a structure, defined by the logical forms of judgment. If perceptual experience is a kind of judgment, and if judgment has certain forms or structures, then the candidates for the categories (the necessary conditions of possible experience) are the forms of judgment. Having identified the candidates, he must show there are necessary conditions of experience. This is the Transcendental Deduction.

The Transcendental Unity of Apperception

The argument of the Transcendental Deduction introduces a fundamentally new concept - the Transcendental Unity of Apperception. This is a formal unity which experience must have. All your experiences belong to one consciousness. When you look out of the window, all aspects of your seeing are united. It is all *your* experience. This formal unity is what makes self-consciousness possible. It makes it possible to think: `these experiences are mine.' This unity makes consciousness of my experience as such possible. Experience has a unity and because of this, I can be aware of my experiences as my experiences. According to Kant, this Trancendental Unity of Apperception (T.U.Ap) is a condition of all experience.

The Necessary Conditions of Experience

This unity is often explained with an analogy. The experience of hearing a tune of twenty notes is not like twenty different experiences each of one note. In this way, all experience is like that of a song. However, the analogy has a misleading aspect - namely that even the experience of one note must be subject to this unity. This T.U.Ap. is not the idea of a self. It is not an entity. It is an abstract and formal or structural feature of experience. Kant realizes that, because the unity is required for any experience, it is not an object of experience. It is not an item which can be experienced. It makes all experience possible, including ordinary awareness of oneself and introspection. When I am aware of my own experience or my own body, the T.U.Ap. is already presupposed. Such experiences cannot constitute this Transcendental Unity. For these reasons, we must not think of the T.U.Ap. as a mystical awareness of a transcendent or noumenal self. It a formal characteristic of experience. It is not awareness of anything. It is a feature and condition of all awareness.

Kant's idea can be explained in a more contemporary way. There is a distinction between these two differences: on the one hand, `Garrett Thomson' and `Michael Lince', and on the other, `I' and `him.' The first pair of words merely indicate impersonally that there are two people. The second pair of words expresses a point of view. It divides the world into I and not I. The difference between the two pairs of words is vitally important to each one of us, because it is a condition of our subjectivity that some impersonal differences can amount to the difference between I and not-I. For Kant, this difference is made possible by the T.U.Ap. Notice that the two words `Garrett' and `I' refer to the same thing. We do not have to assign to `I' a special referent or object.

Kant's approach to the `I' is profoundly new. The Rationalist Descartes takes the `I think' to indicate the existence of a substance, distinct from the body. This ignores an important paradox concerning consciousness - which is that we cannot experience it, because it is experience. Hence, the saying "the I which sees cannot see itself." Kant recognizes this paradoxical point and explains it. According to him, the `I' is not an object of possible experience, because it is a presupposition of experience. Kant does not treat the I as a thing.

The Empiricist Hume also rejects Descartes' reification of the I. He notes that there is no sense impression of the I. According to Hume, all concepts must be derived from sense impressions. Consequently Hume accepts a fundamentally sceptical position about the concept of the I. Kant rejects Hume's scepticism. He agrees with Hume, against Descartes, that the `I' cannot be an object of experience. But he disagrees with Hume that this means that the notion of an `I' cannot be justified. It is justified by being a necessary feature of all awareness.

The Transcendental Deduction

The deduction consists primarily of Kant's argument to show that the categories are indeed the necessary conditions of experience. The deduction also contains a second argument to show that experience must have objectivity features, but that will be a topic of the next chapter. In this exposition, we will concentrate on the B edition of the Deduction, as opposed to the earlier A edition. The cornerstone of the argument is the claim that the Transcendental Unity of Apperception (T.U.Ap.) is a necessary condition of experience. Kant argues that this unity requires that experience is type of judgment. He claims that all judgments require the forms of judgment, or the categories. Therefore, the Unity of Apperception and experience itself would be impossible without the categories. The argument can be summarized as follows

1. All experience must be subject to the T.U.Ap.
2. This requires that experience consist in judgments
3. All judgments must have a form
4. Therefore, the forms of judgment are necessary conditions of experience

The categories are necessary for the possibility of experience. All experience is subject to them, else it could not be subject to the T.U.Ap. Since experience requires the categories, these must be a priori and cannot be derived from experience. The above interpretation of Kant's argument is stated as a piece of conceptual analysis of the requirements of experience, based on section 20. However, Kant states his argument as if he were describing a psychological process (as we shall see later, probably this is not Kant's true intention). He argues (see B 143):

1. If they are to constitute experience, then the manifold of intuitions must belong to one consciousness
2. This implies that they must be subject to the T.U.Ap..
3. This requires that the manifold be synthesized by the understanding.
4. This synthesis is governed by the logical forms of judgment or the categories.
5. Therefore, for experience to be possible, the manifold of intuitions must be subject to the categories .

The Necessary Conditions of Experience

In brief, Kant argues in the Transcendental Deduction that all experience and knowledge must be subject to the Transcendental Unity of Apperception, because otherwise a person's experiences could not belong to one single consciousness. Kant also argues that this unity in experience would be impossible if experience did not conform to the categories. Therefore, he concludes that all experience must conform to the categories and that a priori concepts are possible.

The Schematism

Even after this, Kant sees the work of showing that the categories are necessary as unfinished. He wants to silence the Empiricist objection that these categories are abstractions which have no relevance for empirical knowledge. His strategy is brilliant. First, he argues that the categories have no meaning except for their role in structuring and making experience possible. This leads to Transcendental Idealism and the next chapter. Second, he reveals the role of each of the categories in experience and shows how they make time determinations possible. The categories applied to time are called the Principles. Note that the Transcendental Deduction does not argue that specific categories are necessary. In the Principles Kant shows how each category does this.

In the Schematism, he argues that the categories must be schematized or given a temporal interpretation, so that they can be applied to experience. Why? Empiricists might argue that the categories have no application and they would accuse Kant of being a closet Rationalist. The Schematism is designed to answer such objections. The Empiricist point is: empirical concepts are homogeneous with appearances, because they contain a sensory element. In other words, it is part of the concept of a dog that a dog should look a certain way. However, categories are not homogeneous with appearances. They do not contain a sensory component. It is not part of the concept of a cause that causes should look a certain way. The problem of the Schematism is that there is a case against the categories being applicable to experience. In the Schematism Kant replies to this.

According to Kant time is a mediator between the pure categories and appearances. Because time is the a priori form of sensibility, it is both a priori and sensible. Thus Kant argues that the categories apply to experience only in so far as they determine the necessary temporal features of our consciousness. The categories have legitimate empirical application in relation to time. This is what the Principles will show.

Kant reinforces his reply to Empiricism by rejecting the claim that concepts are images. He says that the schema for an empirical concept is a rule which will enable us to produce an image, but is not itself an image. This claim enables Kant to free himself from the Empiricist problems accounting for abstract ideas.

The Principles

The twelve categories come in four groups of three. So do the Principles, which are the categories temporalized. The purpose of this section is to show how each schematized category is necessary for experience. What is their role? The general answer is that the Principles make objective space and time possible. They make the distinction between objective and subjective time possible, and consequently, are necessary for experience. In this way, they are constitutive of the transcendentally ideal world of things in space and time.

1. The Axioms of Intuition

These correspond to the three categories of quantity: unity, plurality and totality. The corresponding principle claims that all intuitions are extensive magnitudes. Why is mathematics applicable to the natural world? It is not a fortunate accident. Kant's answer is that they were made for each other. According to the Axioms of Intuition, everything in space and time must come under the categories of quantity. Kant's idea is that spatial and temporal properties are extensive magnitudes because they can be added. Because of this, they can be represented with numbers and measured. This principle "alone can make pure mathematics, in its complete precision, applicable to objects of experience." (B206) It seems that the world is amenable to being described precisely with mathematical concepts because it is subject to Kant's axiom. However, for Kant, this is not a question of good fortune. The Principle is a synthetic a priori truth: it expresses a condition of experience which the world (being transcendentally ideal) must conform to. This way the fit is guaranteed.

2. The Anticipations of Perception

This Principle, which corresponds to the three categories of quality (reality limitation and negation) states: "In all appearances, the real that is an object of sensation has intensive magnitude, that is, a degree." Kant is introducing the idea of degrees of quality, which is not

16

a mathematical concept of extensive magnitude. He points out that the qualities of sensations come in degrees that appear continuous, rather than coming in jumps of discrete units, like extensive magnitudes. Probably, Kant is anticipating the later distinction between cardinal and ordinal measurement. An ordinal measurement gives a ranking of things without allowing us to quantify the differences between the things so ranked. Whereas cardinal measurements allow us to say the difference between A and B is twice that of C and D, ordinals do not. Clearly Kant extensive magnitudes are cardinal. The suggestion now is that he claims that intensive magnitudes are ordinal.

3. The Analogies

These principles correspond to the three categories of relation: substance, cause and reciprocity. The analogies are the most important of the principles (they are the topic of Ch. 4). The analogies specify the ways in which objects and events in the world are connected. According to Kant, these connections make time and space possible.

4. The Postulates of Empirical Thought

These Principles correspond to the three categories of modality: necessary, actual and possible. Let's start with the actual: "something is actual if it connects with some actual perception in the accordance with the analogies." (A225) This shows that the actual does not have to be perceived. Distant galaxies and tiny electrons can be actual without being perceived. They can be causally connected to an actual perception and thus belong to the same world, in the same unified space and time.

Given the definition of the actual, those concerning the necessary and possible are easier to follow. By 'possible', Kant means causally possible, as opposed to logically possible. Many things which are logically possible are not causally possible. For example, it is not a logical contradiction to suppose that a man might jump over a huge building, but is not really or causally possible. In this sense, the possible is defined in terms of the Analogies. Similarly for the notion of necessary; the causally necessary is not the logically necessary.

Conceptual and Psychological

The cumulative conclusion of the Metaphysical and Transcendental Deductions, and the Principles is that the categories are the necessary conditions of experience. However, it is not always clear whether Kant is stating conceptually or psychologically necessary conditions for experience. The point has some importance.

Often it appears that Kant is trying to articulate the psychology of our experience. For example, when he refers to synthesis, it seems that he is describing a cognitive process which yields experience as a product. When he claims that certain forms are a priori, he seems to be making the claim that they are imposed upon experience during this processing. Or, he seems to be saying that the categories are inherent in our human faculties, which implies that the a priori forms of experience are part of the human psychological make-up.

There is another (non-psychological) way to understand Kant's a priori. We can see Kant as trying to articulate the *conceptually* necessary conditions of any possible experience. In this case, the a priori forms are not psychological conditions of human experience, but conditions which any experience must conform to, because of the inherent nature of experience itself. Many passages in the Critique support a more psychological reading of Kant. However, such an interpretation would make his overall theory untenable for two reasons. First and foremost, the psychological reading requires a strong interpretation of Transcendental Idealism, which is incompatible with Kant's analysis of objectivity. These are the themes of the next chapter.

Second, Kant demonstrates that the categories are necessary conditions of experience in order to show how synthetic a priori truths are possible in science and mathematics. That is the point of the enterprise: to explain how necessary truths that are not analytic are possible (to use that explanation later in the critical evaluation of metaphysics). However, it is doubtful that the psychological interpretation of the a priori permits us to explain this. Features of human psychological make-up cannot be used to explain, for example, why the world must consist in causally related objects in space and time. You cannot use the empirical to explain the necessary. The idea of human psychology already presupposes a spatio-temporal and causal framework. It presupposes what it is supposed to explain.

For these reasons, when we can, we should try to understand Kant's main conclusions without the psychological idiom when we can, and without pretending that he does not employ that idiom. It is preferable to understand Kant as making conceptual claims about the necessary conditions of any experience. For example, when Kant says that space and time are a priori, we must take him as saying that these are conceptually necessary conditions of any possible experience, rather than psychological conditions of human experience.

18

3

Objectivity and Idealism

Kant is probably the first philosopher to understand clearly the nature of objectivity. At B142 he claims that a judgment is objective means that if it is true, then what is affirms is so, no matter what the state of the subject is. In other words, its truth or falsity does not depend on the person.

The Refutation of Idealism makes a similar point, namely we must perceive external objects that exist independently of us. Kant thinks that the world of objects in space and time is real. Objects exist even when they are not perceived, and they would exist even if there were no humans around. Kant rejects the central claims of the idealist Berkeley, who denies the existence of material things. More radically, Kant also denies a fundamental claim of Empiricism, that we can only perceive our own ideas. Rejecting it, Kant argues that we directly perceive objects in space and time, which exist independently of us.

These realist strands are an important part of Kant's philosophy, but they seem to contradict his Transcendental Idealism, according to which objects in space and time are merely phenomena. In other words, they are not things as they are in themselves or noumena. This means that spatio-temporal objects are ideal, in some sense. Kant even calls them 'appearances'.

How should we reconcile transcendental idealism with Kant's clear belief in the objectivity of spatio-temporal particulars? Kant asserts both:

- The objectivity thesis: the world consists of objects in space and time which exist unperceived and independently of perceivers and,

- The transcendental idealist thesis: the world, which consists of objects in space and time, is in some sense transcendentally ideal.

Both claims are indispensable to the Critique, and yet they look deeply inconsistent. Resolving this contradiction takes us right to the center of the Critique; it shows the deep novelty of Kant's insight.

Objectivity

The Transcendental Deduction contains a second argument (sections 17 -19 in the B edition). The first and major argument aims to show that the categories are necessary for experience. The second argument concludes that the Transcendental Unity of Apperception (and therefore experience itself) requires objectivity. In other words, experience must be of an objective world consisting of things which exist independently of our perception of them. Kant thinks that the idea of an object which exists independently of our perception is a necessary condition of experience.

According to Kant, this idea of an object prevents our modes of knowledge from being arbitrary (A 104). Because of it, experience is rule–governed and has a unity, without which experience would be impossible. For example, we do not perceive redness and then heat. Instead, perception has a structure: we perceive an object as red and hot. The perception of red and hot are united in the object. Kant calls this the objective synthetic unity of apperception and sometimes the Transcendental Object.

In the B edition, Kant says that when we judge that the red object before us is hot, the objectivity of the judgment is expressed by the copula 'is'. The judgment asserts that the object is red no matter what the state of the subject is (B142). When we judge that an object is circular, we judge that it really is circular, even if it appears to be oval from some angles.

Kant argues that objectivity and the Transcendental Unity of Apperception are two sides of the same unity (A 105). Both are required for experience and both require the categories. In other words, the possibility of self-consciousness requires objectivity. This point is not easy to grasp. Let us explain it in two steps.

1) Objectivity.

Kant has already argued that seeing is like judging; to see is to judge that some thing is P. This means that we judge that it really is P and not merely that it seems to be P. In other words, perceptual experience can be mistaken. This requires a distinction between how thinks look and how they are. For example, the circle seems oval from an angle, but really it is circular. Objectivity requires and is implied by the distinction: seems/ is.

2) Self-consciousness.

If I am having an experience, then I must be able to think "I am having this experience." In order to be able to have that thought, there must be a distinction between how things seem to be to me and how things really are. In other words, self-consciousness requires the distinction between how things seem and how they objectively are.

We should not confuse this idea of objectivity with that of a noumenon. Kant distinguishes them (See A 253). The notion of a Transcendental Object or objectivity is a structural or formal feature of all perceptual experience. It permits us to distinguish between how things seem and how they are. On the other hand, `noumena' is part of Transcendental Idealism. It is the empty, limiting concept of reality as it is absolutely or in of itself, without any reference to the necessary conditions of experience.

Kant's notion of objectivity is an important philosophical advance. Objectivity is obviously a problem for Empiricism, which claims both that all concepts must be derived from sense experience, and that we can only ever perceive our own ideas. It is difficult to see how the concept of something independent of, or apart from, experience can make sense on these Empiricist assumptions.

Kant develops this theme of the need for objectivity features in experience in the Analogies. In the Second Analogy, he argues that, without the category of cause, experience could not be of an objective world, and there could be no Transcendental Unity of Apperception and hence no experience. Kant argues that the distinction between the subjective time sequence of our own perceptions and the objective time sequence of events is necessary for experience.

The Refutation of Idealism

In the Refutation of Idealism, Kant argues that we are directly aware of external objects which exist independently of our perceptions of them. In so doing, Kant distances himself from earlier philosophers who held that we can only ever be directly aware of our own ideas. Kant says that he has turned the game played by idealists against itself. Idealism assumes that the knowledge of our own inner experiences is more certain than any belief we could have about the external world. Kant rejects the heart of this assumption by arguing that we can only be aware of our own experiences if we are directly aware of external objects. The existence and knowledge of things outside me is necessary for my awareness of my own experience. Kant tries to bury Descartes' assumption that the experiences of a solipsistic mind would be indistinguishable from a mind which perceived objects. Kant rejects the assumption central to the Cogito that I can have an immediate and certain knowledge of my ideas.

Kant's argument is as follows:

1. I am conscious of my own experiences in time
2. All time perceptions require something permanent in perception
3. This permanent is either a perceptual experience or external objects which are not perceptions.
4. The permanent in perception cannot be a perceptual experience
5. Therefore, the perception of outer objects is a necessary condition of self-consciousness.

The crux of Kant's argument is premise 2. Kant's point is that we can only date an inner state in relation to a framework of outer things which are permanent. Premise 4 asserts that even a relatively permanent perception itself requires an objective time position, and so it requires a permanent which is distinct from itself. In other words, we cannot assign a determinate date to an experience or inner state by appeal to further inner states.

With this one argument, Kant distances himself from the Empiricists, especially Berkeley's claim that objects are merely collections of ideas (see B 142, B 276 and A 820). He also rejects Locke and Descartes' thesis that objects exist behind a veil of perception, because he is argues that we are directly aware of the existence of outer objects, rather than just ideas in the mind (B 277).

Transcendental Idealism

How can we reconcile Kant's views about objectivity with his Idealism? Transcendental Idealism is the claim that objects in space and time are transcendentally ideal. In other words, things in space and time are phenomena and not noumena.

What does this mean? It is best start with the main reason why Kant is sure that Transcendental Idealism is true. He knows that there are synthetic a priori claims about the world, and that these must have some explanation. As we have seen, the explanation has two pillars. First, the necessary conditions of experience. Second, the claim that the world must conform to those very conditions. But, why must it so conform? Kant's answer is Transcendental Idealism. The world of things in space and time consists of phenomena and not noumena. The world is relative to the conditions of experience, i.e. it is phenomenal. For otherwise, it would not be experiencable. Kant is indicating an inherent condition or relativity in our notions of objects and reality. This implies that the world is not absolute: it does not consist in things as they are in themselves, without reference to any conditions. In other words, the world is not noumenal.

For Kant, the notion of noumena is empty. The necessary conditions of experience are parameters. Any claim to metaphysical knowledge that goes beyond those boundaries will be senseless. This is because the categories have no meaning except in relation to possible experience. Therefore, noumena do not form a reality, separate from things in space and time. There is the idea of things in space and time as they are noumenally, that is as they are without reference to the necessary conditions of experience. It is the idea of an absolute viewpoint on things. But this idea is an empty limiting concept.

a) The point of the theory

Transcendental idealism has two important roles:

1. It explains how we can know a priori that the world actually conforms to the necessary conditions of experience, which is vital for explaining synthetic a priori truths.

2. It prescribes the limits of knowledge; Kant claims that space and time and the categories only have meaning in relation to the objects of possible experience, i.e. to phenomena and not to noumena. This is the basis for Kant's attack on metaphysics in the Dialectic.

i) The application problem

Transcendental Idealism is required to explain how synthetic a priori truths about the world are possible. Citing the necessary conditions of experience is not enough. We need the second pillar too: we need to show that the world conforms to those necessary conditions. How do we know that the world does so conform? Transcendental Idealism means that it must. In a simple, radical move, Kant makes the notion of reality relative to the necessary forms of experience. This reveals an inherent relativity or qualification in the concept of reality. By negation, this implies the empty idea of absolute reality (not relative to these necessary forms)- the concept of things as they are in themselves.

So explained, Transcendental Idealism is compatible with the objectivity thesis. Claiming that the form of the world depends on the form of any possible experience does not make the world dependent on perceivers or perceptions. There is an important difference between saying:

A) the formal character of objects depends on the formal
   character of any possible experience, and
B) objects depend for their existence on perceivers.

A), unlike B), does not make the existence of objects depend on any perceivers. According to statement A), spatio-temporal objects would still exist even if there were no perceivers. According to statement B), they would not. A) is compatible with Kant's objectivity thesis; B) is not. A says that the notion of reality is relative to certain conditions. B says that it is relative to perceivers.

Now we can see the difference between Kant and Berkeley . Kant asserts (and Berkeley denies) that objects exist independently of our perceptions. And Berkeley asserts (and Kant denies) that we can only perceive our own ideas. For this reason, Kant claims to be an Empirical realist;   he thinks that spatio–temporal objects are real. They are objectively real, because they do not depend on us for their existence. They are transcendentally ideal because they are relative to the necessary conditions of experience.

ii) Prescribing the limits

In the Transcendental Deduction (section 24),   Kant argues that the categories have no meaning apart from their role in experience. The saying 'concepts without intuitions are empty' applies to the categories, because they are no more than rules which define the form of experience. This implies that they have no meaning beyond that use. In other words, they have meaning only in application to experience and the object of possible experience. This means that the concept of noumena is empty. Kant says that it leaves 'open a space which we can fill neither through possible experience nor pure understanding.' (A289/B345) This is the basis of Kant's criticisms of metaphysics. All of this means that we should not think of noumena as (non spatio temporal) objects. Noumena are not an unknowable realm of objects beyond space and time. To think in that way would be to fall into the error of metaphysics.

Noumena and phenomena are not two different realms of reality.

There is only one world, namely things in space and time. There are two viewpoints on it: the normal view point of possible experience, the phenomenal, and a God's eye or absolute viewpoint, the noumenal. The latter is no more than the empty idea of the unconditioned.

b) Problems for the Strong

Ever since the Critique first came off the printing press, some readers have taken Kant's idealism to be a close variant of Berkeley's. According to this strong interpretation of Transcendental Idealism, (a) reality consists in non spatio-temporal noumena, and (b) phenomenal objects in space and time, or appearances, are merely products or constructs of human experience. Our knowledge is confined to phenomena.

(This strong interpretation is quite different from the weaker or milder one I have given up to now. The strong one claims that noumena are objects; the milder one denies this. The strong version affirms that phenomena are subjective ideas; the mild version denies that.)

This strong reading conflicts with two of the central aims of the Critique. First, it implies that noumena are real. To think that reality consists in non spatio-temporal noumena requires us to apply the categories beyond the bounds of possible experience. Kant's criticism of Rationalism is precisely that one cannot do that. Second, it denies the objectivity thesis. If objects in space and time are merely constructs from human experience, then they are not objective. However, as we have seen, the objectivity of claims about the spatio temporal world is a major theme running throughout the Critique.

To see how this strong interpretation persists and yet conflicts with important parts of the Critique, let us look at two models which require it.

i) The glasses

The first is a pair of glasses. Through rose colored spectacles, the whole world looks rose colored. According to this model, the categories and space and time are similar, except that they are like a priori spectacles, which we can never take off. They are lenses. We have to view the world through the lenses of the a priori forms and what we see are consequently only appearances.

This analogy misrepresents Kant, for the two reasons mentioned above. First, it treats noumena as real. Who wears the glasses? It must be a non spatio-temporal noumenal person. What are the objects which cause our perception? They are noumenal too. Second, it treats things in space and time as ideas, thereby denying the objectivity thesis.

25

According to the analogy, what are objects in space and time? Merely ideas in our minds. In conclusion, this analogy requires the strong interpretation.

ii) The factory

The second problematic image is the factory. According to it, Kant wants to affirm that a person is a psychological factory which receives empirical intuitions from an object. The factory then stamps these sense data with the forms of space and time. It then combines these intuitions, synthesizing them with the categories to form an experience of a spatio-temporal world.

This factory model is really a more sophisticated version of the glasses analogy. It suffers from the same problems. It treats noumena as real. To see this, ask: <u>who</u> is the factory doing the synthesis? It cannot be an empirical human being. For this would make nonsense of Kant's project of explaining the a priori. You cannot explain the a priori in terms of the psychological processes of humans. This does not make sense, since humans are part of the empirical world. One cannot explain the a priori forms of the empirical world through the psychology of beings who are a part of that world. That psychology already presupposes space, time and causality. In other words, the analogy requires a noumenal factory. The factory model involves a piece of noumenal psychology and it implies the strong version of Transcendental Idealism.

Walker says: "The phenomenal world is a construction which our minds effect by working on the data they receive and interpreting these data in accordance with the principle which govern their thinking." This interpretation of Kant requires the postulation of a noumenal mind (because the phenomenal mind is part of what is constructed). In this way, it runs against the grain of the first Critique.

iii) Psychological

Now we can explain a point from the previous chapter more completely. Psychological readings of Kant's a priori imply the strong interpretation of Transcendental Idealism. They will suffer from the problems of that interpretation. First, the claim that <u>we</u> impose the forms upon the world makes the existence of objects dependent on us humans. It thereby renders Transcendental Idealism incompatible with the objectivity thesis. Secondly, a psychological explanation of the a priori requires a positive notion of noumena, as we saw in the factory model.

This means that to maintain the weak form of Transcendental Idealism, which is compatible with the objectivity thesis, we must interpret Kant's notion of the a priori in a purely conceptual, as opposed to a psychological, way. It also means that when Kant explains the a priori psychologically, he is committing himself to the strong version of Transcendental Idealism. Any psychological slant to the claims about the necessary conditions of experience requires a strong version of Transcendental Idealism, which will be incompatible with the objectivity thesis.

Which of Two?

These points highlight the costs and benefits of the strong versus the mild version. The strong interpretation fits many passages of the first Critique. For example, 'objects are nothing but representations'(A 371); space and time are `in us';`what we call outer objects are nothing but mere representations' (A 30). Moreover, Kant often explains the a priori as a psychological claim, and this requires the strong interpretation of Transcendental Idealism.

However, there are also passages in favor of the mild interpretation. For example, we have Kant's claims that the notion of a noumenon is not the concept of any kind of object and is simply an empty, limiting concept (A 255/7). There are Kant's claims that spatio–temporal objects exist independent of our perceptions of them, which entails that, after all, they are not literally representations. The all important point is that the weak interpretation makes the major theses of the first Critique more consistent. It reconciles Transcendental Idealism and the objectivity thesis and makes it more compatible with his own criticisms of metaphysics. We may conclude that, in so far as we can, we should read Kant as embracing the mild version of Transcendental Idealism, which is a more plausible and interesting view.

In the B edition of the Phenomena and Noumena chapter and the Concepts of Reflection, Kant displays an ambivalent attitude towards the notion of a noumenon. He wants to say that such a idea is empty, but at the same time that it is possible. He says it is a concept 'which cannot be reckoned among the possibilities, although must not for that reason be declared to be also impossible' (A290/B347). All of this is more complicated because Kant's moral views seem to require a strong interpretation of Transcendental Idealism. At least, they require that we be able to think of ourselves as noumenally free. If noumena is an empty, limiting concept, how can such a thought have content? The answer lies in Kant's moral theory.

4

Cause and Consequence

Causation is an important concept. It permits us to explain and predict events and gather evidence for the unobserved. However, both Rationalism and Empiricism have problems with it. Notoriously Hume attacks the rationalist conception of causation at the cost of embracing a radical scepticism. Kant is usually credited with replying to Hume's sceptical position, without falling back into Rationalism.

The Rationalist Idea of Cause

There are two aspects to the rationalist notion of cause against which Hume was reacting. First, the Rationalists thought that the effect was necessary given the cause. Given a complete specification of its cause, the effect has to happen. One might say: the cause already contains the effect. The Rationalists tended to think of causation on a model of logical implication: given the premises, the conclusion has to follow. The second aspect of the Rationalist view of cause: they held the principle of sufficient reason that everything must have a sufficient cause why it is so and not otherwise.

Hume's Fork

Hume's sceptical attack is based on his fork according to which

28

all judgments are either judgments of fact or judgments of relations between ideas. Today we would say that all meaningful sentences are either empirical (based on sense observation) or analytic (based on definitions). Hume's fork apparently shows that the justification of any judgment must be based either on reasoning from definitions or on sense experience, which consists in receiving impressions.

Hume's attack on causation consists in applying this fork at three levels. First, the scope of the causal relation. Hume argues that the claim `all events have a cause' cannot be justified. It cannot be justified empirically, by observation, because no-one can observe all events. Neither can it be justified by reason, because it is not an analytic truth. `All events have a cause' should not be confused with `all effects have a cause.' The latter is an a priori truth, because it is analytic, or true by definition. The former is not. Thus, Hume concludes that the Rationalist Principle of Sufficient Reason cannot be justified.

Second, the nature of the causal relation. We assume that causation involves the idea of a necessary connection between events. Hume thinks that this idea of a necessary connection is without justification. It cannot be justified empirically: there is no impression of such a necessary connection. All we ever perceive are events following one after the other. We do not perceive any connection between them. Therefore, the idea cannot be justified with reference to our sense impressions, according to Hume. The idea cannot be justified by reason either. Any two events are logically separate. There are no logical relations between them. They are discrete.

Third, reasoning using the causal relation. We use the causal relation to infer inductively. We see that in the past A has always been followed by B and conclude the next A will also be followed by B. Hume argues that this pattern of inductive reasoning can never be justified. Just because the sun has risen every day up to now does not necessarily imply that it will rise tomorrow. He argues for this inductive scepticism first by arguing that inductive reasoning presupposes that nature will continue in the same way in the future. It assumes that nature is uniform. This assumption cannot be justified. It cannot be justified empirically by induction. We cannot say that because nature has been consistently uniform in the past, it will continue to be uniform in the future. This would merely beg the question.

Kant's Trident

The essence of Hume's fork is that it only offers two alternatives:

either propositions are a priori and analytic, or else they are synthetic and empirical. The claim that every event must have a cause fits into neither of these two options. Over this last point Hume and Kant are agreed. However, Kant rejects Hume's fork, because he thinks that the causal claim is a synthetic a priori truth. He thereby rejects Hume's view that causation cannot be justified.

In the Second Analogy, Kant supports this conclusion by arguing that the category of cause is a necessary condition of experience. In so doing, he challenges a basic Empiricist assumption: if a concept is not derived from experience, then it cannot be justified. If Kant can show that the idea of causal connections is a necessary structural feature of experience, then it can be justified even if it is not derivable from sense experience. It is not derivable from sense perception precisely because it is a requirement of experience.

The argument of the Second Analogy is notoriously difficult to follow. However, it helps to remember that all the categories play a two–fold role: one, they provide the necessary unity of consciousness, and two, they give our experience objectivity features. For Kant these are two sides of the same unity, a unity which is necessary for experience. Causality also plays this double role.

To be more specific, in the Analogies this double role of the categories means that we must be able to distinguish the subjective temporal sequence of our experiences and the objective sequence of events. We need to distinguish a succession of perceptions from a perception of succession. That distinction is a requirement of experience. This is the first step of the argument of the Analogies.

The second step is that the categories are needed to make the above distinction possible, because space and time themselves cannot be perceived. We cannot make objective time determinations by dating events in relation to time itself, because we cannot perceive time itself. We only perceive changes in time.

We find these two steps in the specific case of the Second Analogy, together with a third step specific to that Analogy.

- The first step: we need to distinguish a subjective succession of perceptions from a perception of objective succession. This is a requirement of experience.

- The second step. All our perceptions are successive. What characteristics of our experience enable us to count perceptions that succeed each other as the perceptions of objects that do not? For example, we look at the top and then the bottom of a house. These perceptions are of different parts of the house which coexist. They are not perceptions of events. What feature of experience enables us to place events in an objective time order? Kant's answer is that our perceptions lack or possess the feature of order indifference. When I perceive the coexistent parts of a house, my experiences could have occurred in the opposite order, i.e., they possess the feature of order indifference. When I perceive an objective change, like the movement of a boat downstream, my perceptions lack this feature of order indifference; my perceptions could not have occurred in a different order. Kant claims that the concept of an objective alteration depends on the use of the idea of a necessary order of our perceptions.

- The third step: Kant affirms that the order of our perceptions is necessary implies that the appropriate changes in the object are causally determined.

Accordingly, Kant's argument can be put as follows:

1. The distinction between the subjective sequence of perceptions and the objective sequence of events is a necessary condition of any experience.
2. This distinction can only be made empirically in relation the necessary order of perceptions
3. If the order of our perceptions of a change is necessary, then the order of the change itself is causally determined.
4. Therefore, causation is a necessary condition of any experience.

From this conclusion, we can deduce that all events are caused, but only given the extra premise that the world must conform to the necessary conditions of experience (i.e. Transcendental Idealism). Any event without a cause could be not experienced. Therefore all events must have a cause. In the above argument, premise 1 is a conclusion of the Transcendental Deduction. Kant argues for premise 2, by claiming that neither time itself, nor the mere order of our perceptions are adequate to make the required distinction.

Kant is arguing that objective time is made possible by causation. E1 occurs before E2. We cannot think of that objective determination in relation to absolute time. Kant's idea is that cause makes that determination possible, because a cause cannot come after its effect. E1 is before E2 if and only if either E1 causes or is simultaneous with the cause of E2 (simultaneity is the topic of the Third Analogy). Cause-effect makes before-after possible. The direction of time is made possible by the irreversible and asymmetric nature of the causal relation. This interpretation of Kant, made famous in the 20th century by the philosopher of science Hans Reichenbach, is the forerunner to the contemporary causal theories of time. Causal theories of time aim to specify a physical basis for time relations through causality, without presupposing temporal notions.

Kant's Answer to Hume

Earlier we saw that Hume's scepticism about cause has three dimensions: he thinks first that 'all events have a cause' cannot be justified; second, that the idea of a necessary connection between events is unjustifiable; and third that induction cannot be justified. Kant's Second Analogy deals directly with the first dimension. We now have to consider the other two.

a) Necessary Connection

We are in outer space where there is no appreciable gravity and no air resistance. A brick with a mass of 3 kg is traveling, with an acceleration of 2m/s, towards a window 10 meters away . The window can exert a resistance of 2N. Will the window break? If there are no other relevant factors, it seems that we must conclude 'yes.' We can put this deduction as a simple syllogism:

1. A body with a mass of 3 kg and an acceleration of 2m/s is moving towards a window at a distance of 10m.
2. The resisting force of the window is 2N
3. Force equals mass times acceleration
4. There are no other relevant factors.
5. Therefore, the force of the moving body is greater than that of the resisting body.

The window breaks. With this example, we can see that a complete relevant description of the cause, plus a specification of the relevant causal laws, plus the claim that there are no other relevant factors (or that the system is a closed one) will logically entail the description of the effect. With these kind of entailments in mind, the Rationalists claim that the effect is already contained in the cause, because given the cause, the effect has to happen.

Hume's rejects the notion of a necessary connection between events, arguing, first, that there is no such sense impression, and second, that events are separate happenings. Thus there is no logical necessity that, given the one, the other must happen. Hume redefines cause in terms of constant conjunction, replacing the idea of necessary connections with that of mere regularities. A causes B just when B regularly occurs after A (there can be no idea of A making B happen). For Kant the concept of a cause is that of a change which takes place in accordance with a rule or a law. It is a sequence of events which is rule governed. This renders Kant's view of the nature of causation more similar to the Rationalist one than to Hume's. Kant can thereby distinguish a causal relation from a mere regularity. On Sundays the newspapers are larger than the usual dailies. A few hours after these Sunday newspapers come out, vicars give sermons. There is a regularity, but not a causal connection. According to Kant, this is because the two events are not connected by a causal rule. On the other hand, if you drop a ball, it falls. This is not merely a regularity, but also a causal sequence: the two events are connected by the law of gravity.

However, despite the distance between him and Hume, Kant is not a rationalist about causation. Kant insists that specific causal laws must be discovered empirically, even though we can know a priori that all events do have a cause. Rationalists, however, treat specific causal laws as necessary truths which can discovered by deductive reasoning from the Principle of Sufficient Reason. In comparison, Kant does not think that particular causal laws can be deduced directly from the Second Analogy. Particular causal laws are not necessary conditions for experience. This much is clear. Less clear or more difficult is Kant's final position about the status of the causal laws, the discussion of which we must postpone until the chapter on science.

b) Induction

What is Kant's solution to Hume's problem of induction? Well, first what is Hume's problem? Hume notes that our beliefs about the future are generalizations based on observed constant conjunctions in the past. In the past A has always been followed by B, so when we see A we expect B to happen. However, Hume argues that there is no rational justification for this kind of inductive inference. For this radical conclusion, Hume argues that inductive inferences assume that the course of nature continues uniformly. It just presupposes that the future will be like the past. Hume thinks that this assumption cannot be justified. There is no reason for believing that the course of nature is uniform, that it will continue in the same way in the future as it has done in the past. Hume's argument is:

1. If our beliefs about the future are justifiable then the supposition that nature will continue uniformly can be rationally justified.

2. This supposition cannot be rationally justified.
3. Therefore, our beliefs about the future are not justifiable.

Hume's argument for premise 2. can be seen in terms of his fork: beliefs can only be justified by the evidence of the senses or by deductive reasoning. The principle of the uniformity of nature cannot be justified in either of these two ways. Not on the basis of past observations (up to now, the future has always resembled the past, therefore it will do so in the future). Such an argument presupposes the principle and cannot be used to justify it. Not on the basis of reason: there is no deductive proof of the uniformity principle, for this would require that the Principle is an analytic truth, which it is not. Because the principle cannot be established either by deductive reasoning or by inferences based on past experience, Hume concludes that we have no reason to believe that the principle is true. Induction cannot be justified.

Kant does not answer Hume by claiming that the Principle of the Uniformity of Nature is a necessary condition of experience. The Second Analogy only tells us that every event must have a cause. It does not tell us what particular causal laws are, nor that they will remain the same in the future. To cut a long story short, Kant's reply to Hume on induction would be as follows. The analogies constitute principles to which any event must conform. The physical laws which govern specific changes can be deduced from these overarching principles, but only given the required empirical information, for example about the existence and nature of matter. According to this explanation, physical laws are not synthetic a priori necessary conditions for experience, but neither are they empirical generalizations. They have an intermediary position; they have both an empirical and an a priori element.

On the basis of this, we can give a Kantian reply to Hume's scepticism regarding induction. Because causal laws are more than just empirical generalizations, nature will be uniform. Nature must behave in law-like ways, and for this reason inductive inferences sometimes work. They enable us to predict successfully when they track a causal regularity. Despite all this, we need to empirically investigate the world to find out what those causal regularities are, because causal laws have an empirical element. More on this in chapter six.

The First Analogy

We can conceive of two kinds of changes. First, changes in which a thing remains but its properties change; for example, the leaves change their color; the tree grows. Second, there are changes in which new things come into existence and old things pass away. In the First Analogy, Kant tries to prove that in all changes substance is permanent. He argues that all changes which appear to be of the second type are really changes of the first type. In other words, all changes are alterations to the properties of substance. There are no changes of the second type which are not also changes of the first kind, because there is no absolute creation or destruction of substance. Therefore, the amount of substance cannot change.

The First Analogy is similar to the Principle of Conservation of Matter. However, it is not identical to it because Kant does not argue that substance is matter. The relation between the Principles and the a prior part of physics will be explained in chapter six.

Kant argues that the principle of the First Analogy is a synthetic a priori truth. It is not analytic, because it gives us information about the world. It is not empirical, because it is a necessary truth. Kant's argument for this conclusion is similar to the argument for the Second Analogy. The first part consists of the same steps.

First, experience requires the distinction between the subjective and objective (how things appear to me and how they are). This distinction is a requirement of the unity of consciousness. It means that, in principle, we must be able to separate the subjective time sequence of our perceptions from the objective sequence of events. Our perceptions change constantly, but some of those changes represent real changes in the world and others do not.

Second, objective judgments about when changes occur cannot be made in relation to an absolute time. Newton's absolute time is not an object of possible experience (see Ch. 5 and 6). We cannot rely on it as a fixed absolute grid or axis for dating events, even implicitly.

Third, this means that there has to be something permanent aspect of experience in relation to which we can make judgments about the objective timing of events. This, of course, is substance. Therefore the category of substance is a necessary condition of experience. Accordingly, Kant's argument is as follows:

1. Experience requires that we be able to distinguish within experience between the subjective and objective time sequences.
2. This distinction cannot be made in relation to absolute time
3. This distinction can only be made in relation to the notion of substance as a permanent.
4. Therefore, the concept of a permanent substance is a necessary condition of experience

In addition, according to Transcendental Idealism, all events in the phenomenal world must conform to that category, because otherwise they would not be objects of possible experience. Given this and premise 4, the first Analogy follows:

4. The concept of a permanent substance is a necessary condition of experience
5. All events in the phenomenal world must conform to the necessary conditions of experience.
6. Therefore all events conform to the principle of the permanency of substance

The crucial premises are the second and third. Strawson and others ask: Why should we accept that third premise? Perhaps a relatively permanent background of objects would serve instead of the notion permanent substance. In which case, the third premise would be false. This is how Strawson and others have argued against Kant.

This line of objection misrepresents Kant in two ways. First, Kant is not making the epistemological point that to know the date of events we need natural clocks, or a background of regularity. Kant's point concerns the meaning of objective time determinations. Second, we cannot just assume that there is a background of relatively permanent objects because the nature of the empirical world is what is in question. Otherwise, one is presupposing Transcendental Realism.

The spirit of Kant's argument is more like this: experience must be structured around the concept of a permanent substance because experience has to be of objective events. But the temporal objectivity of events requires a grid or axis in relation to which they have a date. However, this grid or axis cannot be time itself, because that presupposes an absolute conception of time. What plays that role in experience is the concept of permanent substance. Since that is a necessary condition of experience, and since all changes in the world must conform to those necessary conditions, then all changes are alterations in substance.

Kant has another argument for the absolutely permanent. At A186 he says that the creation of new substances would make the unity of time impossible. The idea is that permanent substance represents the unity of time. `The unity of time' means the fact that an event occurring at any time has a determinate temporary relation to any other possible event. If a new substance could be created, then the unity of time would be impossible, and there would be two unrelated time sequences. But without the unity of time, there could be no unity of experience.

1 If experience is to be subject to the Transcendental Unity of Apperception, then there must only one time sequence
2. If substance could be created or destroyed then there would be more than one time sequence.
3. Therefore, if experience is subject to the Transcendental Unity of Apperception then no new substance can be created or destroyed.

All change must be considered as the alteration of the permanent substance. No change can be considered as the creation or destruction of substance, because a change in the quantity of substance would destroy the unity of time. In other words, the concept of a change in the quantity of substance can have no application in experience, and in this sense the universe is a closed system.

The Third Analogy

In this Analogy Kant claims that objects must interact causally in order for them to coexist in space. As already seen, Kant thinks that the unity of the natural world is the counterpart of the necessary unity of consciousness. The unity of the natural world requires the unity of space and time. Space and time would be a disunity if there were any part of space or time which did not have a determinate spatial or temporal relation to every other part of space or time. In the Third Analogy Kant argues that since space and time cannot be perceived, their unity must be known in terms of the unity of their contents. In other words, the unity of space and time must be represented by the causal interaction of objects.

Kant's claim in the Third Analogy is that objects not causally related to other objects cannot be thought of as having a definite date. Such objects could not belong to the same temporal sequence as other objects. An unrelated object could not be simultaneous with other objects because it could not be part of a single time sequence. What Kant has in mind is not difficult to grasp. When we see a distant star explode, we can know at what time this happened only because we can know details about how the star stands in causal relation to other objects on Earth and our own perception. It is only because the star causally interacts with other objects that we can give it a definite date.

5

Space and Time

In our exposition, we jumped forward missing out Kant's treatment of space and time in the Transcendental Aesthetic. Now that the two central pillars of the Critique are clearer, let us return to the Aesthetic. Remember that Kant has to explain how synthetic a priori truths are possible. He does so by arguing that experience is subject to certain necessary conditions, or a priori forms, and that the natural world must be subject to those same conditions. Given this, not surprisingly, the main claims of the Aesthetic are:

1. Space and time are Transcendentally Ideal
2. Space and time are a priori forms of experience
3. Mathematical judgments are synthetic a priori truths

Kant's idea is that because 3 is true, 1 and 2 are also true. These are not the only themes of the Aesthetic; Kant also argues that space and time are intuitions.

Space as A Priori

Kant claims that space and time are the a priori forms of sensibility or intuition. Our experience of objects must be spatial and temporal. Given this and given Transcendental Idealism, objects must be located in space and time. In the Metaphysical Expositions he gives two arguments for the a priori nature of space. First, he argues that space is not an empirical concept derived from experience. We could not derive our idea of space by abstracting it from our experience of adjacent objects, because to represent objects as adjacent requires an idea of space. Thus space is a priori. Second, Kant argues that we can imagine space empty of objects, but not the absence of space itself. From this, he concludes that space is a priori, presupposed by our awareness of outer objects. Space is logically prior to the objects which exist in it.

Kant has two other arguments for the claim that space is a priori, or a necessary condition of experience. The first is the argument from geometry, which we will examine below. The second might be called the argument from objectivity. Experience must have objectivity features, because this is a necessary condition of the Transcendental Unity of Apperception. Therefore, sense experience must be of objects. Additionally, objects must be spatio-temporal. Their identity requires it. Imagine a part of the universe consisting of two molecules. What makes them two is that they cannot occupy the same space at the same time. The identity and individuation of objects requires their spatio-temporality. Kant makes these points in criticizing Leibniz in the Amphiboly of Reason. If experience must be of objects and objects must be spatial, then space is a necessary condition of experience.

The Argument from Geometry

According to Kant, geometry contains synthetic a priori truths about space. For instance, compare the statements:
(1) A triangle has three sides.
(2) The angles of a triangle add up to 180 degrees.
Both statements are necessary truths, and are a priori However, (1) is analytic and, according to Kant, (2) is synthetic. It is not part of the definition of a triangle that it must have 180 degrees. We can only deduce that the triangle has this property given the Euclidean nature of space. Therefore, statement (2) tells us something about the character of space. It is an a priori judgment which gives us knowledge of the world.

In the Transcendental Exposition of Space, Kant argues that the only possible explanation of the synthetic a priori truths of geometry is his own theory. Our perception of objects must be spatial, and all objects must conform to this spatial requirement because this is how experience is ordered. He says that space is not a property of things in themselves: space is transcendentally ideal because otherwise we could not explain how we have a priori knowledge of it.

Non-Euclidean Geometries

Developments in non–Euclidean geometry suggest that geometry does not consist in synthetic a priori judgments. Non-Euclidean geometries describe curved spaces. For example, the surface of a sphere is a curved two dimensional space. In Euclid's geometry, the fifth axiom says parallel lines meet at infinity. Non-Euclidean geometries deny this. The historical development of non-Euclidean geometries does not tell against Kant's theory. He denies that Euclidean geometry is analytic, which implies that non-Euclidean geometries are logically possible. The problem is that Kant thinks that it is a priori that space is Euclidean, whereas in fact, it is an empirical truth that it is non-Euclidean. Einstein's theory of general relativity predicts that space will curved by matter with mass. The theory was confirmed when astronomers measured the exact location of star during the eclipse of the sun. Einstein's theory had predicted that the space around the sun would be slightly curved by the huge mass of the sun, and that, as a consequence, the star would appear to be in a slightly different position. As a result, the actual shape of space appears to be an empirical question. This is a serious challenge to Kant's claim that geometry is synthetic a priori.

These recent developments apparently show that Hume's two pronged fork is more correct than Kant's trident. In other words, what Kant thought of as a body of synthetic a priori truths are really either a set of analytic truths or a set of empirical claims. On the one hand, analytic geometry consists of formalized systems which model spaces with different topographies. This is a priori and analytic. On the other hand, the investigation of which models best describes physical space is empirical. The physics of space would consist of synthetic and empirical truths. Neither of these (analytic geometry and the physics of space) contains synthetic a priori propositions. Thus, Kant is wrong.

There are two responses on Kant's behalf. First, although the shape of physical space is an empirical question, this does not demonstrate that there are no synthetic a priori propositions about space at all. There might be others. Kant certainly thinks that, because he argues that the Axioms of Intuition are synthetic a priori. Everything in space and time must come under the categories of quantity. Space is necessarily quantifiable. According to Kant, these claims are not analytic or empirical. It is not analytic that space and time should have these general characteristics; it is not true by definition. It is not an empirical truth either because space has to be like that to guarantee the applicability of mathematics to space. Kant concludes that the axioms are synthetic a priori truths about space and time. So, although some of the claims that Kant thinks of as synthetic a priori turn out to be empirical, this is not a conclusive argument for the claim that there are no synthetic a priori truths about space and time.

Second, that geometry can be formalized does not imply that it must consist of analytic propositions. Kant claims that existential propositions cannot be analytic. Pure logic cannot show us what exists. (This principle forms part of his argument against the ontological proof for God's existence; he claims that `God exists' cannot be an analytic statement). However, the axioms of geometry contains existential propositions. For example, `there exists at least two points'; `if L is a line then there exists a point not on L.' Some systems, like geometries, set theory and arithmetic contain existential propositions about what exists (such as `there is a null set'). These existential propositions cannot be analytic, irrespective of whether they can be formalized or not. Kant would say that these proposition are synthetic a priori.

Space and Time as Intuitions

Leibniz and Newton had fundamentally different views of space and time, which are debated in Leibniz's letters to Clarke. Newton conceived space and time as absolute, infinite wholes. Any region of space is a part of the one unlimited infinite whole. Similarly for time. They are absolute: they exist independently of, and prior to the things which are in them. This view has many implications. For example, according to Newton's theory, it is meaningful to suppose that a finite material universe could have been differently situated in absolute space. A finite material universe could have been situated 10 meters to the left from where it actually is located. Similar statements apply to time and, in particular, the universe could have been created earlier or later than it in fact was with respect to absolute time. Absolute motion is motion with respect to absolute space for a period of absolute time. Thus, for Newton's theory, it is meaningful to suppose the whole finite material universe might move with respect to absolute space.

Leibniz rejects this absolute conception of space and time. For him, space is not a container which exists logically prior to and independently of physical bodies. He argues that the existence of matter is logically prior to the existence of space: physical objects or forces happen to be ordered spatially, and space is nothing over and above these spatial relations. It is merely a system of relations. Leibniz argues that space and time are reducible to the spatio and temporal relations between things. Apart from these relations, space and time are nothing.

This relational view of space and time has several consequences.

First, that it is meaningless to suggest that the universe could have been created in a different position and can change position in space. For Leibniz, there is no absolute space, and an object can change position only relative to another object. It cannot change position in relation to absolute space. For Leibniz, space is nothing over and above the spatial relations between objects, and consequently, it is meaningless to suppose that all objects could have been differently situated. Similarly for time: according to the relational theory it is meaningless to suppose that the universe could have been created earlier or later, because time is nothing over and above the temporal relations between events. There is no absolute time. There can be no time before the creation of events. Because he denies the concepts of absolute space and time, Leibniz also rejects the idea of absolute motion. For Leibniz's theory, there can be no such thing as motion against the background of unmoving absolute space. The motion of any physical body must be relative to the motion of other physical bodies.

Leibniz argues for the relational theory by claiming that Newton's view contravenes the Principle of Sufficient Reason. Leibniz says that God could have no possible reason for creating the universe in a different region of space or at a different period of time. Since everything must have a sufficient reason, it cannot make sense to say that the universe could have been created earlier or elsewhere in space; these cannot be genuine alternatives, contrary to the claims of the absolute theory.

Kant forwards a view which agrees with neither the absolute nor the relational view. He carves out a position midway between Leibniz and Newton. On the one hand, Kant affirms that space and time are themselves intuitions, rather than concepts. In claiming this, he denies they are relations. He affirms that space and time are unique, infinite individuals: all spaces are parts of the one whole space, and similarly with time. In this way, Kant's position looks Newtonian.

(This is what Kant means by claiming that space and time are themselves intuitions. Often Kant uses the word `intuition' to stand for the faculty of sensibility, as opposed to that of understanding. However, he also employs the term `intuition' to mean something like the product of sensibility (in contrast to `concept'). In this sense Kant uses the term, when he claims that space and time are intuitions. He means that they are individuals or particulars.)

In the Aesthetic, Kant gives two arguments to show that space is an individual or an intuition, rather than a concept or a relation. First, he argues that there is only one space. Different spaces are simply parts of the whole. Therefore, different spaces are not comparable to instances of a general concept. Thus space is not a concept but an intuition. Second, Kant argues that space is an infinite given magnitude, and therefore it is not a concept but an intuition. In the Prolegomena, Kant has another argument against Leibniz's relational theory, which is called the argument from incongruous counterparts. According to this there is a difference between a left handed and a right handed object (such as a glove or a particle with spin) which cannot be accounted for on the relational theory.

On the one hand, as we have just seen, Kant argues against Leibniz's relational view of space. On the other hand, he also rejects Newton's absolute view in two ways. First, in his discussion in the Analogies, Kant claims that absolute space and time cannot be perceived. One cannot measure, or even think of, change or motion against a background of absolute space and time. Change requires a background of other objects. This is a vital premise in the arguments of the Analogies. Space and time need a physical basis, and this is provided by the categories at work in the world. Second, Newton's theory treats space and time as transcendentally real. According to Kant, all objects of possible experience must be in space and time; therefore, space and time themselves are not objects of possible experience. Moreover space and time are infinite, and for this reason, they are not objects of possible experience. Thus to treat them as absolute entities is to think of them as transcendentally real. In opposition to this, according to Kant, space and time are transcendentally ideal features of the natural world and not noumena.

Kant's claim in the Aesthetic that space and time are intuitions should be compared with his claims about space and time in the Analytic of Principles. The general characteristics of space and time, such as their unity and their metric nature, are made possible by various categories. To ignore this contribution of the categories would be to think of space and time as absolute entities with their characteristics already given. This would fall into the error of accepting Newton's theory of space and time. In this way, the Analytic supplements the Aesthetic.

Time

Kant argues that time is the a priori form of sensibility, and that it is transcendentally ideal. Kant's views on time mirror his theory of space, except for two differences. First, he says that whereas space is the a priori form of outer intuition, time is the form of inner intuition. In so far as our awareness is directed inwardly to our own experience, we are aware of a temporal series. When awareness is directed to outer things, then it must be a spatial awareness. In other words, experience itself must be temporal, but objects must be both spatial and temporal.

The second difference between Kant's exposition of space and time is this: geometry is the a priori science of space, but it is not clear in the Aesthetic that there is a parallel a priori science of time. Kant does claim that there are synthetic a priori truths about time, such that it is one–dimensional and metric, but it seems there is no parallel to geometry for time. However, there is some textual evidence, later in the Critique, for arguing that Kant regarded arithmetic as a body of synthetic a priori based on time.

Arithmetic

According to Kant arithmetical propositions like `7+5 =12' are synthetic a priori. Most people would think that they are analytic. Kant argues that they are not. Kant would put the issue in the following terms: is it part of the definition or meaning of `7+5' that it must be equal to 12? He says we cannot logically deduce from the concepts of seven and plus five that this equals twelve. He says that it is more obvious with large numbers that such propositions are not analytic. In other words, Kant would argue that it is not part of the meaning or definition of `7 plus 5' that it equals the cube root of 1728.

Perhaps, we can add a little bit more clarity to Kant's insight with a contemporary distinction between sense and reference. The phrases `the planet Venus' and `the morning star' refer to the same thing, but they do not have the same sense or meaning. Two phrases with the same reference do not necessarily have the same sense or meaning. Kant might argue that `7+5' and `12' do not have the same sense, and for this reason, the statement `7+5 =12' is not analytic. Yet, he might argue that the two phrases `7+5' and `12' must have the same reference, and for this reason, the statement is a priori.

Echoing our discussion of geometry, an Empiricist would argue that Kant is mistaken because arithmetic is analytic. This argument would consist in showing that all of arithmetic is reducible to the logic of set theory. To do this, we should show that all propositions about numbers can be reduced to ones about the natural numbers. Second, we define zero and the mathematical idea of succession in terms of sets. With these two notions defined, we can generate any natural numbers, because any natural number is either zero or a successor of 0. The key definitions are:

- 0 is the set which has the null set as its only member.

- the successor of any number n is the set of all sets that when deprived of a member come to belong to n.

In this manner, all natural numbers can be generated and arithmetic is reducible to the logic of set theory.

This argument against Kant is not decisive. The problem with it is that it assumes that the axioms and theorems of set theory are all analytic. As we saw when discussing geometry, Kant thinks that existential proposition cannot be analytic. Set theory and Peano's axioms for arithmetic contain what are apparently existential propositions. For example, Peano's axioms postulate the existence of the number zero and from that postulate the other numbers. In set theory, we assume the existence of the null set (the set which has no members) and define the number zero in terms of it. From that one set, we can construct all the other sets which define the natural numbers. The point is that these axioms make a priori assumptions about what must exist. Kant would argue that they must be synthetic.

Problems of Interpretation

There are several problems regarding the Aesthetic, which we should briefly mention.

1) The Factory Model

In the Aesthetic Kant seems to be postulating a factory model of cognition. To put it crudely, the model says that the thing in itself immediately affects sensibility causing a manifold of empirical intuitions which are ordered spatio temporally and then are synthesized by the understanding, in accordance with the categories, to yield experience of spatio-temporal objects. Kant puts forward this data-processing model in the Aesthetic.

We have already mentioned some of the problems with his model. Let us briefly return to these points. First, a very important aim in the Critique is to explain how the empirical world has certain features a priori. The problem concerning the factory model is that it clearly cannot fulfill that aim. The a priori features of the empirical world cannot be explained by the psychology of phenomenal beings. This is because such beings are already a part of that world and subject to space and time. The existence of humans already presupposes space and time and the categories. Consequently, the psychology of human beings cannot be used to explain how synthetic a priori truths about the empirical world are possible. We are part of what is to be explained. Beings in time do not make time.

Therefore, the factory model requires noumena. According to it, Kant is describing a cognitive process of noumenal beings. For example, space and time are the a priori forms of the faculty of sensible intuition - who is the subject that has that faculty? According to the current interpretation, we should reply 'the noumenal self.' However this reply violates another important claim of the Critique- the unknowability of noumena. Worse, under this interpretation, he is applying the categories beyond the realm of possible experience. The main aim of the Critique is to show that we cannot meaningfully use the notion of an object beyond the bounds of possible experience. (In chapter three we mentioned another problem: namely that the noumenal version of the factory model makes the phenomenal world depend on us and thereby contradicts Kant's claim that objects are objective).

Conclusion: the factory model conflicts with some major claims of the Critique. This cannot be a reason for denying that Kant advances this model; for he does affirm it. These problems, however, are a reason for looking for an alternative way to understand him.

2) Empirical Intuitions

The notion of an empirical intuition, sometimes called the manifold of sensible intuitions, is a problematic concept, which needs to be handled with care. Most definitions of the concept fall back on the factory model: sensible intuition is the faculty of immediate cognition, which presents the matter or the raw data of knowledge to be processed by the understanding into knowledge. Empirical intuitions are the raw sense data, which has to be processed. Such explanations seem to require the noumenalism inherent in the factory model.

There is a different problem with the notion. Intuitions without concepts are blind. This means that they are possible objects of experience, because they would not be subject to the Transcendental Unity of Apperception. Intuitions without concepts are not even objects of immediate cognition, because they are not subject to the required unity of consciousness. Kant rejects the Empiricist idea of sense-data experience. Therefore we should not think of empirical intuitions as sense-data. There is a simple alternative that avoids these problems. It is to think of the manifold of empirical intuitions as an aspect or facet of any experience. Any experience must consist an intuitive or particular and a conceptual or general element. However, these two elements are inseparable from experience itself.

6

Science:
Objectivity Without the
Absolute

From 1755 to 1770, Kant had an enormous and varied teaching load. He lectured 20-30 hours a week on subjects as diverse as geology, astronomy, natural history, anthropology, mechanics, theoretical physics, and different branches of mathematics. In this early period, Kant had a very active interest in the natural sciences. At the age of 23 in 1747, he wrote a treatise called the *True Evaluation of Dynamic Forces*, a discussion of whether the force of a body in motion is equal to mv (as Descartes held) or mv squared (as Leibniz held). His doctoral thesis was about fire. He wrote several essays about the wind, the tides, the aging of the Earth, earthquakes and other scientific matters. In 1755 he published anonymously the book, *A General Theory of the Nature and History of the Heavens*. To explain the origin of the solar system, kant proposed his nebular hypothesis. He believed that matter was being formed into solar systems by the force of gravity. He wrote: "Creation is never complete; it is still going on." He is credited with being the person to first propose that some of the lights we see at night are galaxies, or huge clusters of stars, thereby anticipating Laplace.

This chapter is a brief parenthesis in our examination of the first

Critique. We need to understand Kant's mature views on science, and this involves a closer look at the *Metaphysical Foundations of Natural Science* (1786) (MFNS for short), as well as peeking forward to the *Critique of Judgment* (1790). In the MFNS, Kant presents an argument similar to the Schematism of the first Critique in which the categories yield the Principles by being temporalised. The difference is that in the MFNS, the Principles are materialized to yield the most general physical laws (i.e. the mediating concept is not time but matter). The *Critique of Pure Reason* gives us the formal a priori conditions for any experience. Given that the world must be relative to those conditions, it explains how there are pure synthetic a priori truths about the world. However, the Critique does not aim to give us a theory of physics. For example, the First Analogy tells us that substance cannot be increased or decreased. However, we should not just assume that this substance is matter. According to Kant, what the world is made up of is an empirical question which must be settled by experimentation, and not by a priori theorizing. Likewise, the Second Analogy concludes that every event must have a cause, but it does not tell us what particular causal laws are at work in the world. That is an empirical question.

However, Kant thinks that physics has an a priori element. By this he does not mean that the most abstract principles of physics are necessary conditions of experience. He means rather that physics has a structural framework and in this way, it is not entirely empirical. Kant calls this a priori element `general natural science.' More specifically, physics is the study of matter. What is matter? Kant defines it as what is movable in space. However, this abstract definition is not enough. Kant has to show how the concept of matter is applicable to the natural world of our experience. We might say that Kant seeks an operational definition of the concept. For, on the one hand, matter cannot be defined in terms of Newton's absolute space, which gives no empirically serviceable criteria for what matter is. On the other hand, Kant must avoid the instrumentalist approach of Hume and Berkeley, who deny that physics describes an objective physical reality at all. For Kant physics is more than just a complex tool for predicting patterns in our sensations. It describes reality. Thus, Kant has to show how the concept of matter is objective, without making it absolute.

Viewed in these terms, Kant's aim is to show how it is possible that physics describes the objective world. He does this by stating the necessary conditions for the application of the concept of matter - those conditions which are needed to guarantee its applicability to the objects of possible experience. Of course, the physics that Kant examines is largely Newtonian. However, Kant is not trying to prove Newtonian physics by showing that its laws are necessary for experience. On the contrary, Newton is more part of the problem than the solution. By tying his physics to an absolute conception of space, Newton divorces it from a working empirical basis and opens the door to the scepticism of Hume and Berkeley. Kant's remedy is to show how the concept of matter finds application without appeal to the absolute conception of space. In this way, Kant aims to show how it is possible that physics describes an objective world. This enterprise does not detract from the empirical character of science. The laws of nature may be a priori, but not in the sense that they are necessary conditions for experience, and not in any sense which denies the need to investigate them empirically. The most general laws of nature are conditions for the objective application of matter.

A more orthodox way to characterize Kant's project is as follows. In the First Critique, he needed to temporalize the categories to show their relevance and role for experience. As a result, the categories are converted into the Principles that, as we saw, make objective space and time possible. That is their role in experience. The *Metaphysical Foundations of Natural Science* is concerned with a similar process for matter. He aims to show that the Principles, when materialized, state the necessary conditions for the objectivity of physics.

For this reason, the *Metaphysical Foundations of Natural Science* is set up so that the four chapters of the book to correspond to the four groups of categories and the Principles, as follows:

CATEGORY	PRINCIPLE	MFNS
1. Quantity	Axioms of intuition	Phoronomy
2. Quality	Anticipations	Dynamics
3. Relation	Analogies	Mechanics
4. Modality	Postulates	Phenomenology

1. The Phoronomy

For Kant the fundamental property of matter is motion. In the First Critique, the Axioms of Intuition are supposed to guarantee that objects are describable mathematically, because their spatio-temporal properties are extensive magnitudes which can be added to each other. In the MFSN Kant now wants to make the same point about the motion of bodies. Velocities can be added together. For this reason, they can be represented as magnitudes and described mathematically and thus they can represented spatially - velocities as lines and bodies as points.

In this first chapter of the MFNS, Kant gives a new slant to his argument against the Newtonian concept of absolute space. In the Critique Kant argues that space and time are unities. There could not be two spaces unrelated to each other. Any area of space is related to any other area of space (which means that objects could move from one to the other). The two areas can be included together as one larger region of space. However, this process of inclusion does not mean that we can assume the reality of an all-inclusive, infinite space. According to Kant, this idea of an absolute, infinite space as a whole is an ideal, a regulative idea, but not an object of possible experience. The concept of absolute space has no possible application in experience. Consequently, neither does that of absolute motion.

2. The Dynamics: Impenetrability

In the Metaphysical Foundations of Dynamics, Kant explains further requirements for the application of the concept of matter. The claim that matter is the movable in space also requires that it fills space. This leads to the impenetrability of matter. Matter is the difference between empty space and space which is has something in it. This may sound very obvious, until we recall the historical context. Many Rationalist philosophers prior to Newton, like Descartes and Leibniz, thought that empty space was impossible. First, well, what is empty space? Nothing, of course. But, to say that it is nothing is to say that it does not exist. Second, for Descartes, space is nothing more than spatial extension and extension is the essential property of all matter. Empty space is impossible because a property cannot exist without the substance which it is an attribute of.

It seemed that the only way to affirm the possibility of a vacuum was to adopt Newton's view of space which makes space an infinite, absolute object. Since Kant thinks that all objects must exist in space, thinking of space itself as an object cannot be right. So how do we deny Descartes without embracing Newton? We cannot make material substance equivalent to space. For, as we have just seen, this leads to the impossibility of a vacuum. Furthermore, it seems that there has to be something to be extended in space. In other words, matter cannot consist merely in its spatial properties; there must be some other quality of matter which has those properties.

For these reasons, Kant defines matter in terms of the power to exert a force. An object resists anything which tries to occupy the space which it is in. It is impenetrable. Consequently, two objects cannot be at the same place at the same time. However, Kant rejects the idea of absolute impenetrability as an ultimate property of matter. He argues that this idea falls foul of the same principle as Newton's absolute empty space: namely that it is an empty concept because it is not something we could ever encounter in experience. Instead, Kant argues that the impenetrability of matter should be explained in terms of the forces of repulsion.

Kant's main claim in the Metaphysical Foundations of Dynamics is that the notion of attractive and repulsive forces make possible the general concept of matter. They make it possible because they are required to ground the concept of impenetrability, which itself cannot be fundamental or absolute.

3. Mechanics: Matter and Mass

In the third chapter, the Metaphysical Foundations of Mechanics, Kant explains the notion of moving forces and the quantity of matter or mass. Kant defines the quantity of matter in terms of acceleration and force. Again Kant is concerned with the preconditions of the concept of matter, which he thinks are given by three laws of mechanics. These laws are similar to Kant's Analogies and to Newton's laws of motion, but they are not the same as either. They hold an intermediate position between the two, as necessary conditions for the applicability of the concept of matter as mass. Only in this sense are they a priori, and as such, Kant tries to demonstrate them.

1) The law of Conservation: In all changes of corporeal nature, the quantity of matter remains unchanged.

2) The law of Inertia: Every material change has an external cause (the velocity of bodies will remain constant unless they are acted on by an external force).

The word `external' precludes inner causes or living forces causing changes. All changes must have a cause that can be represented mathematically and which obeys the law of conservation of matter. According to Kant, the above principle also precludes the idea of inertial force - the idea that motion will grind to a halt on its own. According to the above law, external causes or force is only needed to cause changes in velocity (acceleration or deceleration).

3) The principle of the equality of action and reaction: In all communication of motion, action and reaction are always equal.

Kant defines mass in terms of momentum (quantity of motion).

How should we define the quantity of matter? We could do that in terms of density and volume. But then we would have to define density without appealing to the concepts of inertia or absolute impenetrability (because these have no application). The alternative is to define mass in terms of quantity of motion (i.e. as a function of the force required accelerate a body).

These points are important. Kant has defined matter as that which moves in space. However, this on its own does not give us an empirically working concept of matter. It does not show how matter is an object of experience, or something real. To do that, Kant needs to show that the concept of matter can have an empirical application without presupposing the Newtonian notion of absolute space. Kant has now solved this problem. He has defined the relevant features of matter without appealing to absolute space. He can admit the relativity of motion without denying the reality of matter, by defining forces and mass in terms of changes in velocity.

4. Phenomenology

Having explicated the role of the concept of force within the a priori framework of physics, Kant can now return to the question of the relativity of motion with more clarity. Newton's first law of motion implies that a body will continue in uniform rectilinear motion unless subject to some force. Forces are necessary to cause acceleration and deceleration. Can we not then use the concept of force to distinguish between absolute and relative motion? Kant replies negatively to this question by distinguishing true and absolute motion. Of two bodies, we can determine which one truly is in motion by measuring the forces. However, this does not mean that the object that is accelerating is in absolute motion with regard to absolute space.

Causal Laws

These explanations of mechanics help resolve a tension in Kant's thought regarding the status of causal laws. According to the standard interpretation of the second analogy, it is an entirely empirical matter what particular causal laws govern events in the world. We can know a priori that there are such laws, but not what they are. The introduction to the *Critique of Judgment* apparently reinforces this view. Kant says that it is a contingent matter whether the causal laws of the world are understandable by us. Judgment requires us to assume that causal laws of nature can be systematized to an unified body, which is understandable by us. However, says Kant, this does not mean that nature itself will comply to judgment's assumption. Again, it seems that Kant is affirming that natural laws are utterly contingent.

This official view of causal laws does not fit well, however, with other things Kant says which imply that causal laws are not merely empirical generalizations. As we have seen, we find a better alternative in the *Metaphysical Foundations of Natural Science*. It is that there are intermediate positions between the pure a priori and the strictly empirical. According to this, these laws are not purely a priori because they have an empirical element (namely the concept of matter) and they are not necessary conditions for experience. Laws like Newton's are only relatively a priori: for instance, we can know a priori the principle of the conservation of matter only given that we know the empirical truth `matter exists'. The important point is that if the general laws of nature are relatively and impurely synthetic a priori, then they are not contingent empirical truths.

According to this idea, the *Critique of Judgment* should not be taken to assert that causal laws are empirical generalizations, but rather that it is contingent whether they are understandable by us, in such a way that they can be unified into a systematic body of knowledge, as science is. This assertion is compatible with the idea that the laws themselves are necessary and universal truths. To return to the theme of induction: according to this interpretation, the uniformity of nature, the claim that the future will resemble the past, which is a presupposition of induction, would be guaranteed as a relative and impure synthetic a priori truth. However, the point in the *Critique of Judgment* is that even if nature is regular and uniform, even if the Bs always follow the As, this is no guarantee that we can grasp those regularities, the laws underlying the Bs and As. Regularity is a different issue from comprehension.

This brief detour into Kant's views on science has been important for stressing Kant's rejection of Newton, which leads him to look for more operational definitions of key physical concepts. This idea is very important now in physics. The need for an operational definition of simultaneity was a key element in Einstein's argument for special relativity. The detour has been important also for introducing the idea of intermediate claims between the pure a priori and the empirical. As we shall see later, this idea (of the relative and impure synthetic a priori) is important for Kant's ethics. We can now return to the *Critique of Pure Reason*.

7

Reason's Critique

The first half of the *Critique of Pure Reason* has explained how a priori knowledge of the world is possible. From this we have a theory of experience opposed to Empiricism. Also, we have gathered the principles underlying Kant's criticism of Rationalism. Kant has established that it is impossible to have knowledge which transcends the bounds of possible experience, because beyond that, the categories have no sense: concepts without intuitions are empty. In the Dialectic, Kant shows how speculative metaphysics falls foul of this principle. Rationalists (such as Descartes, Spinoza and Leibniz) claim to have a priori knowledge of the soul, God, and the universe. They try to apply the categories beyond the limits of possible experience.

Another way to put this: synthetic a priori truths are possible in science and mathematics because they articulate the necessary conditions both of experience and of a transcendentally ideal world. Synthetic a priori truths in metaphysics are not possible because they do not do this. Kant shows that the Ideas of reason satisfy neither of those two conditions.

However, the Dialectic is more than a refutation of Rationalism. It is a critique by Reason of itself. Reason is the faculty which makes inferences. In the Dialectic Reason works out why it gets embroiled in metaphysics, even after it has been shown that the metaphysical project is impossible. In other words, Kant gives a diagnosis to reveal why Reason falls into such errors. In brief, Reason searches for a complete explanation of everything. Because of this, it seeks the unconditioned -

that which does not depend on any further condition. The mistake is to expect that the world should conform this demand for the unconditioned. The demand is impossible because the unconditioned is not an object of possible experience. Consequently, nothing in the phenomenal world could ever met that demand. In this way, the Ideas of Pure Reason overstep the limits of sense. According to Kant, this produces an illusion which continues to deceive us even after it has been exposed, because this illusion is an inevitable product of Reason.

To counter-balance this illusion, Kant describes the proper theoretical function of Reason. Reason is not wrong to search for a complete explanation. The error is to assume that anything in the world could answer that search. Rather we should treat the Ideas of Reason as maxims which guide our inquiry. The error is to suppose that these heuristic maxims are constitutive of experience and give us a priori knowledge of the world.

The Paralogisms

Descartes tries to prove the existence of a simple, non-physical substance, the soul. His premise is the 'I think'. Kant opposes this, claiming that the 'I think' is just the formal unity of consciousness. It is a necessary condition of experience, and therefore cannot designate any object or self. What is presupposed by any experience cannot be an object of experience. Descartes is mistaking a formal feature of experience for the awareness of a substance, the soul.

The Transcendental Unity of Apperception cannot be an object of experience, because every experience must be subject to this unity. In this Kant agrees with Hume that there is no impression of the 'I'. However, according to Kant, the search for the 'I' is pointless, because any seeking must be done by the 'I' and so what is sought is already presupposed. It is not an item found in experience. Thus, Descartes mistakes 'the unity of experience for the experience of a unity'.

The Paralogisms are fallacious arguments in support of rational psychology. There are four of them. The first affirms that the 'I' is a substance. By definition, a substance is a subject of predicates and is not a predicate of any other subject. I am not a predicate. Therefore, I am a substance. Kant says this argument rests on an empty notion of substance. The concept of substance can only have meaningful application to objects of possible experience. The 'I think' is not an object of possible experience and so, in the above argument, the notion of a substance is misused because it lacks empirical content. In this way, to say that the I is a substance is to make an empty statement without content, which palms us off with the pretense of an insight. Because the statement 'the I is a substance' is without content, we cannot use it to prove the immortality of the soul, nor to distinguish the self from matter.

The second Paralogism asserts that the soul is a simple. The actions of a simple cannot be regarded as the actions of an aggregate. The soul fits this bill. For example, a body is not a simple because the motion of a body can be regarded as the combined motion of its parts. On the other hand, the thoughts of a person cannot be regarded as combined thoughts of an aggregate, because the thoughts of one person must belong to a single consciousness. Therefore the soul is a simple. Kant rejects this argument on the ground that the transcendental unity of consciousness does not designate an object and, therefore, does not refer to a simple. According to Kant, Descartes confuses the unity of consciousness with the richer idea of a simple soul. The unity of consciousness is a necessary condition of experience and itself cannot be an object of experience. But the notion of a simple has meaning only in application to the objects of possible experience and, therefore, the claim that the soul is a simple is vacuous and without meaning. For this reason, Descartes cannot use this claim to try to establish his mind/body dualism.

The third Paralogism asserts that a person is that which is conscious of its numerical identity through time, and that the soul is such a thing. Kant replies that the claim that the soul is conscious of its numerical identity through time merely expresses the necessary unity of consciousness. This unity of consciousness is not an object. Hence for Kant, the claim that the subject is numerically identical through time is empty. In fact, at A 363 Kant says that even if there were soul substances, there could be no guarantee that a person might not consist of as many souls as he has experiences rather than one soul. There can be no guarantee that one person has only one soul. The point here is that the notion of an identical soul can not work because it contains no criteria for identity, unlike the notion of a spatio-temporal object. My experience could inhere in 2000 souls, but the experience would still be mine because it is subject to the Transcendental Unity of Apperception.

In conclusion the basis of Kant's arguments in the Paralogisms is that rational psychologists inflate the 'I think' to yield conclusions that do not follow. Kant argues:

1. The unity of consciousness or the 'I' is not an object of possible experience

2. The categories have meaning only in application to objects of possible experience.

3. Therefore, we cannot apply the categories to the 'I'

Thus, we cannot meaningfully claim that the I is a simple, numerically identical, non-material substance. In this way, Kant tries to defuse the Cartesian assumption that the 'I' has a purely inner reference to a mental substance.

Kant does not deny that I have empirical knowledge of myself. I can have knowledge of my own body, but this is like the ordinary knowledge we can have of any external object. I can also have knowledge of my own experiences through introspection or inner sense, but this too is empirical and not a priori knowledge.

The Antinomies

The Antinomies consist of a thesis and an antithesis which are apparently contradictory propositions that can be supported by equally valid proofs. The arguments for both the thesis and antithesis assume a certain view of Reason. When we accept this view of Reason, we find ourselves entangled in the Antinomy, having equal reason to assert the thesis and its contradiction.

For Kant this shows us that we must reject the view of Reason on which both sides of the Antinomy are based. Kant claims that this view of Reason entails Transcendental Realism, and that once we adopt Transcendental Idealism, the antinomies are solved. Thereby Kant tries to reveal why speculative metaphysics is so seductive and to uncover its error. He tries to go beyond the claim that metaphysics is empty by showing that it involves a contradiction. In the process he provides an indirect proof of Transcendental Idealism.

Kant advances four antinomies:

1. *Thesis:* The world has a beginning in time and limits in space.
Antithesis: The world has no beginning in time and no limits in space.
2. *Thesis*: Nothing exists except simples or composites made of simples.
Antithesis: There are no simples.
3. *Thesis*: Natural events have free as well as natural causes.
Antithesis: All causation is natural.
4. *Thesis*: There belongs to the world an absolutely necessary being.
Antithesis: No absolutely necessary being exists either in or outside the world.

The First Antinomy

The thesis claims that the world is finite both in space and time. In the case of both space and time, the argument is based on the proposition that a completed infinity is impossible. Hence, the world must be finite.

The antithesis argues that the universe must be infinitely extended in both space and time. In both cases, the argument is based on the proposition that a finite universe cannot be explained. For time: it is impossible for the world to have a beginning. Before the first event, there existed nothing at all, and so there was nothing to explain why the world began exactly when it did. Thus, the world cannot have a beginning and must be infinite in time. Similarly, for space: if the world were finite in space, it would be limited by the empty space around it, but empty space is nothing at all, and therefore there is nothing for the world to be limited by. Thus, it must be infinite in space.

Kant's explanation of these arguments is in terms of the unconditioned. The unconditioned does not require further explanation. Reason demands that the unconditioned exists because if the conditioned is given then the unconditioned is also given. In other words, Reason demands a complete and exhaustive explanation of an event, and thus it presupposes the existence of something which does not require explanation, namely the unconditioned.

We now can explain the shape of all the arguments of the first Antinomy. The unconditioned must exist. The unconditioned is either the universe as a finite whole or as a infinite whole. The thesis argues that the unconditioned cannot be an infinite whole, therefore it must be the finite whole. The antithesis argues that the unconditioned cannot be a finite whole, therefore it must be the infinite. In this way the antinomy is generated.

The solution to the Antinomy is to deny the premise shared by the arguments for both the thesis and antithesis. This premise is the assumption made by Reason that something must exist which corresponds to the idea of the unconditioned (B 501). Once we reject this claim of Reason that the unconditioned should exist, the antinomy can be diffused. This faulty view of Reason can be replaced by one which sees Reason as setting us an indefinite task rather than making an imposition on the world. Reason sets a directive rather than making a claim as to what exists.

Kant says that the unconditioned can never be experienced (B

511). According to Transcendental Idealism, the world of things in space and time is phenomenal and consists of objects of possible experience. Reason's demand that the unconditioned must exist implies Transcendental Realism. Once we reject Transcendental Realism and replace it with Transcendental Idealism, we can see that Reason's demand can never be satisfied. Reason claims that the unconditioned exists and that it is either the infinite series of events as a whole or a finite series of events as a whole. Kant claims that the notion of the whole series of events (whether finite or infinite) is empty. There is no possible experience to which these words could apply. For instance, no experience could count as the discovery of the first event, and consequently, the notion of the whole finite series of events has no possible application. Similarly no possible experience could ever justify us in using the words `the infinite series of events as a whole.' At A483 Kant claims that experience can only justify us in using the term `whole' in a comparative sense. In referring to the series of events as a whole, we use the term `whole' in a non-comparative sense. This use has no application in experience and hence is empty. In the words of Strawson, "we must not think of the endless task of investigation as a task of investigating the endless."

The Second Antinomy

The problem and solution of the second Antinomy is essentially similar to the first. The thesis claims that simples (or indivisible atoms) exist. It is impossible for a composite to be made up of aggregates itself made up of aggregates and so on without end. Therefore, there must be indivisible simples. The antithesis argues the impossibility of composites being made up of simples, because every part of a composite occupies space, and space is infinitely divisible. Anything which occupies space is infinitely divisible and cannot be made up of simples.

Both arguments assume that there must be an unconditioned. The thesis argues that it must consist in simple atoms, because a completed infinity is impossible. The antithesis that it must consist in the infinitely divisible because simples are impossible. Kant's solution to the Second Antinomy is to reject the unconditioned, i.e. the assumption that matter in space is given either as a finitely or as an infinitely divisible whole. Matter in space is indefinitely divisible and presents us with an endless task of investigation. Once again this endless task of investigation should not be confused with a task of investigating the endless.

Freedom

The antithesis of the third Antinomy makes the deterministic claim that there is only natural causation. The thesis affirms that there is both natural and free causation. To solve this antinomy Kant must reconcile the doctrine of determinism with the idea of freedom.

The principle that every event has a cause is a necessary condition of experience. Therefore, according to Kant, each and every phenomenal event is determined by its phenomenal or natural cause. However, Kant also claims that we can view our actions as free. He claims that this is a precondition of morality.

Kant's solution to this antinomy is that we can regard ourselves and our actions in two ways: first, as causally determined phenomena and secondly, as noumena that do not belong to the spatio-temporal world. In other words, an action can be viewed as a natural event determined by its natural causes. Or, it can be viewed as something willed by a noumenal being. Because we can regard ourselves and our actions in two ways, the doctrine of determinism and the idea of freedom can be reconciled and the Third Antinomy can be solved.

According to Kant, moral imperatives apply to rational beings as such. However, moral imperatives apply only to free agents, and as rational beings, we must be free agents and visa versa. This point leads Kant to equate Reason with the Free Will. Free Will cannot be subject to the conditions of time. All temporal events are causally determined, and therefore, in regarding ourselves as rational beings susceptible to moral imperatives, we must regard ourselves as noumena.

Kant's reconciliation of freedom and determinism has some notorious problems. First, a clarification. Kant is not asserting that some phenomenal events have a noumenal cause. As we saw earlier, if we can, we should avoid attributing to Kant an ontological dualism. Phenomena and noumena are not two kinds of things. Noumenal causes are not in addition to phenomenal causes. Rather they are two ways of regarding the same thing.

Second, given this, how can we ever know which natural events are to be regarded as having a free and noumenal cause? Kant affirms that knowledge of noumena is impossible. This means that we can never tell which events should be regarded as having a noumenal cause and which cannot. Hence we can never know when to ascribe moral responsibility or not.

Third, what does it mean to assert that we must think of ourselves as noumena? Kant is careful to claim that we can only think or regard ourselves as noumena and to deny that we can know ourselves to be such. However, if the concept of noumena is an empty, limiting concept, then the thought of our selves being noumena must also be an empty thought. How can an empty thought be any thought at all? Kant's answer would be this: the thought that we are noumenally free beings is empty from the point of view of theory. It acquires a different kind of meaning in relation to the practice of morality.

Lastly, Kant must regard rationality as non-temporal. Otherwise, we could not be free as rational beings. However, we are also committed to seeing rationality in temporal terms, for instance when we reason about events in the world. It is difficult to see how a non-temporal faculty of Reason could ever reason about temporal matters. How could an essentially non-temporal faculty entertain thoughts with an essential temporal content?

Some Concluding Points

The third part of the Dialectic concerns the ideal of Reason: God. After explaining the nature of the idea of God, Kant criticizes the Rationalists for trying to prove God's existence. Since his criticisms of traditional theology need to be contrasted with his own alternative views, which in turn require his moral philosophy, we shall postpone this topic until chapter ten.

Kant's main aim in the Critique is to give a sustained non-empiricist argument against rationalism, thereby transcending both these traditions. The judgments which are most important to science and mathematics are synthetic a priori, and therefore cannot be justified analytically nor by empirical observation. Their justification appeals to two conditions: the necessary structure of experience and transcendental idealism, the claim that the world must conform to that structure. Indeed their sense depends on these two conditions. The claims of traditional metaphysics, which are obviously neither analytic nor empirical, fail to satisfy these two conditions. Hence the difference between science and metaphysics. Metaphysics is impossible not because it fails the two prongs of Hume's fork but because it fails the third prong of Kant's trident.

This is not the end of the story. For there are other types of judgment which are potentially synthetic a priori; for example, those of morality. How can these be justified and explained? We now pass into the second chamber of Kant's thought: the moral. This will be divided into three parts: the first concerns the nature of morality; the second, politics and the third, religion.

8

The Moral Imperative

According to Hume, morality is based on a feeling of sympathy. The general tenor of much of Hume's thought is that our fundamental convictions cannot be justified. Having reached this sceptical conclusion about our ideas of cause, object and self, Hume proceeds to give a naturalistic explanation of those convictions. Hume thinks that philosophers have overestimated the reasoning and cognitive aspect of our nature. Hume's naturalistic explanations are usually based on the more emotive sides of human nature. Hume's view of morality follows a very similar pattern. Ought judgments cannot be justified, but they can be explained, in terms of our feeling of sympathy.

There are problems with this type of view. For example, suppose I do not feel sympathy. In such case, Hume's position seems to imply that I am not under any obligations to avoid harming you. If morality is based on sympathy then unsympathetic people are not under any moral obligations. Furthermore, if morality is so based, then there can be no sense to the claim 'I ought to feel more sympathy.'

Kant sees these problems with a position like Hume's (he was familiar Hutcheson's work, which is similar to Hume's). In opposition to it, Kant distinguishes between hypothetical and categorical imperatives. A hypothetical imperative is conditional on a want; it has the form:

If you want X then you ought to do Y

Kant realizes morality cannot consist of hypothetical imperatives only, because we could escape moral demands by giving up the wants they are conditional on. He thinks morality places inescapable demands on

62

us - for example, not to harm others. Hypothetical imperatives only specify the means to some end. If you do not will the end, then you do not need to will the means, and can thus escape them. The Categorical Imperative cannot be escaped this way. Morality concerns ends.

By claiming that morality is inescapable, Kant does not mean that people will actually do what they ought to do. Rather the point is that one cannot escape that one ought to do it. For this reason, Kant claims that the essence of morality consists in the Categorical Imperative, which has the unconditional form:

You ought to do Y

The categorical nature of morality emphasizes that it is not dependent on individual self-interest and happiness. Someone who tries to show that being moral is in our individual self-interest has not understood morality. Morality is not dependent on escapable self-interest.

The main aim of Kant's moral philosophy is to explain and justify the inescapable binding nature of morality. It is to explain how the Categorical Imperative is possible. Kant does this in *The Groundwork of the Metaphysics of Morals* (1785). This imperative cannot be derived from experience; it is not empirical. Therefore, given that it is not merely an illusion, it must be a priori. He says: "Categorical imperatives require a transcendental deduction because they are synthetic judgments a priori of practical reason."

In the preface to the book, Kant says: "the basis of obligation must not be sought in human nature or in the circumstances of the world in which he is placed, but a priori simply in the concepts of pure reason." Kant thinks that to explain and demonstrate the Categorical Imperative, he must isolate the a priori element of morality. This does not mean that human nature and the circumstances of our lives are unimportant for morality. But these empirical factors cannot explain the inescapable nature of morality. Kant discusses the application of morality to human life the later work, the *Metaphysics of Morals* (1797). Applied morality depends on various empirical factors, primarily the nature of human beings. For the moment, Kant is only concerned with the a priori form of morality, to explain its inescapable nature.

The Answer

The question is 'How is the inescapable nature of morality possible?' Kant answers that the categorical demand of morality is inherent in our being persons with free will. This capacity for freely choosing our actions, Kant calls practical reason. Morality is inherent in the form of practical reason. This is why we cannot escape the demands of morality. It is applicable to all beings with a free-will.

In the first chapter of the *Groundwork of the Metaphysics of Morals*, Kant tries to show that the Categorical Imperative is already part of our normal everyday morality. He realizes that showing this is not a substitute for the transcendental argument which he proposes to give later in the book. Kant thinks that the basis of popular morality is the will. The nature of the will is to freely initiate actions. In this sense, the will transcends the causal chains of nature, and might be compared the act of creation by God: it makes something new. According to Kant, to call an action morally right is to describe the nature of the initiating or original impulse which causes the action. It is the original doing, or the willing of the action, which can be called morally good. What makes the will good is the intrinsic value of what it wills, rather than its consequences. To use an analogy, it is the flavor of that originating impulse which makes the will good, and not what happens later on down the causal chain. The flavor or content of that willing is described by what Kant calls the subjective maxim of the will.

Kant claims that the moral worth of an action does not depend on its effects or consequences. In part, this is because the will is by definition under our own control; the effects of our actions depend on factors beyond our control. Since it is the originating cause, and not later consequences, which makes the action right or wrong, Kant's moral theory is concerned with the motive of our actions. A morally right action must be done for the morally right motive. Kant gives us the example of a shopkeeper. If the shopkeeper refuses to overcharge his customers because this is the right thing to do, then his action has moral worth. The same action done out of prudent self-interest has no moral worth. Kant not mean that keeping prices low merely for the profit motive is morally wrong. Rather it is not morally good. There are plenty of actions which are neither morally good nor morally bad. They are just morally neutral (like drinking orange juice).

Kant expresses the claim that a morally right action must be done for the morally right motive by saying that a good will must act for the sake of duty. Actions which happen to accord with duty are different from those which are actually motivated by a sense of duty. However, the term `duty' is slightly misleading to us, because we usually think of duty as something imposed on us by another person in authority. This is the opposite of what Kant means, because for Kant freedom is the essence of morality.

Another important point which reinforces a rather puritanical reading of Kant is the way he opposes duty with natural inclination or desire. Kant thinks that an action done for the sake of duty, which is caused by a good will, cannot be done out of desire or natural inclination. However, Kant does not claim that actions performed from desire are morally bad; rather they are morally indifferent. Furthermore, Kant does not claim that merely having the desire removes the moral worth from an action.

By `duty' Kant means "the necessity of acting out of reverence for the (moral) law." For an action to be moral, we have to do it because it is the right thing to do, or out of respect for moral values as such. In other words, the subjective maxim of ones action must accord with the moral law or the Categorical Imperative.

We can contrast Kant's view of ethics with Utilitarianism, a developed later by Mill. For a Utilitarian, the point of morality is to increase happiness. The right action promotes more happiness than the alternatives. There are three important characteristics of this view: first, that the only directly morally relevant feature of our actions is their effects or consequences; second, that happiness is the only intrinsic or non-instrumental good; and third that the morality requires us to view our actions impartially. Kant would agree only with the third of these. For him happiness is an intrinsic value, but there are others, such as autonomy and justice. More importantly, Kant denies that our actions are right because they are means to good effects. The rightness of an action act depends on the will.

In summary, Kant's moral philosophy revolves around free-will in three ways. First, we are under an inescapable moral obligation or the Categorical Imperative, because this is inherent in our being free. Second, the essence of morality is that we will in accordance with morality's demand. Third, as we shall see, that demand consists in that we respect the freedom of persons. In other words, morality applies to us because we have a will and it directs our will to respect the will. The will is the precondition, the carrier, and the receiver of the morally right. It is a precondition and the receiver of moral rightness precisely because it is the carrier or bearer of morality. It is because we will that morality applies to us both on the demand and supply side.

Versions of the Categorical Imperative

Before giving a transcendental argument to justify the Categorical Imperative, Kant wants to show what it consists in. He gives four versions, which are supposed to be different formulations of the same fundamental principle. He means that the later versions can be derived from the first version. The Categorical Imperative describes how a perfectly rational being would act. For impersonal rational beings, such us humans, it is an imperative or an ought which prescribes how we should act. However, these versions of the Categorical Imperative state the necessary form of all moral judgments. They do not give us both necessary and sufficient conditions for an act's being moral (they need to be supplemented with the content of morality).

1) Universal Law

Act on that maxim through which you can at the same time will that it should become a universal law. What is the justification for this first formulation? The Categorical Imperative cannot prescribe action on the basis of any specific empirical ends because that would convert it into a hypothetical imperative. Consequently, the only end which the Categorical Imperative can recommend (in the first formulation) is the universality of law as such. The only condition for the Categorical Imperative is the universal nature of the law itself. We might put it like this: the only thing reason can recommend first is rationality itself.

What does this highly abstract principle recommend? First, the law is universal as opposed to particular; the moral law cannot make an essential reference to this particular person, as opposed to that. It means that partiality based on me and mine cannot be a part of morality. Second, it rules out inconsistent willing. I cannot will that other people should not lie to me, and will that I lie to them. I cannot will that all people should be treated equally and then make an exception. This would be a logical contradiction.

There are two kinds of inconsistent willing ruled out in this way. First, maxims which strictly cannot be universalized. They become impossible when universalized. To use Kant's own example, it is impossible to universalize the following maxim: I will borrow money but not pay it back. If everyone had that maxim, money lending institutions would collapse. There could be no lending under such conditions. This kind of maxim generates perfect duties - acts which one must not perform at any time. Second, some maxims are not strictly self-contradictory when universalized, but they are inconsistent with some natural end which a rational person would will. For example, the development of ones talents. These maxims generate imperfect duties - acts which in general one should perform. This distinction between perfect and imperfect duties is important, because in *the Metaphysics of Morals* Kant employs it to distinguish between law and virtue.

2) Respect for Persons

Act in such a way that you always treat humanity, whether in your own person or that of another, never simply as a means but always at the same time as an end. The central idea is that we must respect persons by never using them as instruments for some goal, for example by manipulating them. In part this means respecting the fact that persons are beings with free will which means not depriving them of choice. It also means that one has an imperfect duty to help others.

Kant thinks that this version of the Imperative follows from the first, because the will must be determined by an end. This end must be valid for all rational beings as such, and therefore cannot be based on any desire. The only alternative is that the end be rational nature itself. Moreover, rational nature cannot be merely a means. This is because means exist only for the sake of ends and ends exist merely for the sake of guiding rational beings. Given that rational nature is an end in itself, the second version of the Imperative follows.

3) Autonomy

So act that your will can regard itself at the same time as making universal law through its maxims. This formulation of the Categorical Imperative is similar to the first. There is an important difference of emphasis; it introduces the person as a law-maker or as an autonomous being. For Kant this third version follows from the second. The second postulated rational nature as an end in itself, but what is rational nature? In part, it is the capability to will freely. According to Kant, freedom of the will is the capacity to act according to self-made laws, rather than according to external factors. In this sense, the will is autonomous (as opposed to heteronomous). Thus, when we regard a being as rational, we regard him or her as a law-maker. Combine this idea with the first version of the Categorical Imperative (concerning universality) and you have the third version: regard your will as making universal law.

4) Kingdom of Ends

Act on the maxim of a member who makes universal law for a merely possible kingdom of ends. The idea of this formulation is that each member of a communty of persons should regard his or her maxims as making a law which would govern the actions of all the other members too. Only in this way can a community of rational beings treat one another as ends. By 'kingdom' Kant means a systematic union of persons through common laws. A person is a member of a kingdom when he or she is subject to these laws as well as making them. A kingdom of ends is an ideal. It is a community of persons each one of whom acts autonomously without infringing the autonomy of the others. Each is a person to himself and everyone else. This ideal plays an important role in Kant's political theory.

The Argument

We can represent Kant's overall argument in the Groundwork as follows:

Argument A
1. If we are beings with a free-will, then the Categorical Imperative applies to us without exception;
2. We are beings with a free-will;
3 Thus, the Categorical Imperative applies to us without exception

The argument shows us that there is a Categorical Imperative, and not just hypothetical imperatives. It aims to show us that we are inescapably bound to do what is moral, whatever our desires and ends happen to be.

Kant's argument for the first premise comes in three steps, and is represented in argument B below. The first step is that beings with a free will must also have practical reason. For Kant, 'practical reason' means that our actions can be guided by reasons. If our behavior was not capable of being motivated or governed by principles or reasons of our choice, then we would not be free. Our behavior could not be properly described as free action at all (see premise 1 below).

Second, that we are capable of being moved by reason implies we are rational beings, which in turn means that we are capable of acting in accord with the Categorical Imperative. Kant says: "Will is a kind of causality belonging to living beings in so far as they are rational." k 446 (see premise 2 below). This means that if we are rational beings then the Categorical Imperative is possible (see premise 3 below).

Third, the last step is to show that if the Categorical Imperative is possible then it is binding. By definition, a categorical imperative applies to rational beings as such. Therefore a categorical imperative cannot lay down any particular empirical ends; such ends would only generate hypothetical imperatives. The only end which could be recommended by the Categorical Imperative is rationality itself.

Argument B
1. If we are beings with a free-will, then we have practical reason
2. If we have practical reason, then we are rational beings
3. If we are rational beings then the Categorical Imperative is possible for us
4. If the Categorical Imperative is possible for us then it applies to us without exception
5. If we are beings with a free-will, then the Categorical Imperative applies to us without exception

Kant gives various arguments of this form or type in both the Groundwork and the Critique of Practical Reason. For example, he argues for the above conclusion in relation to the first formulation of the Categorical Imperative, presumably on the grounds that the other versions can be derived from it.

Kant also has a more direct argument for this thesis that free-will implies the Categorical Imperative at the beginning of the third chapter of the Groundwork. We must conceive the will as a cause of our actions. This requires that the will act according to some law. But the law in question cannot be the laws of nature, because the will is supposed to be free. The will must operate according to self-imposed laws, and the only such law is the Categorical Imperative.

Note that Kant is not claiming the moral imperative is inherent in the concept of reason. This is because reason per se might only direct us to act in accord with hypothetical imperatives, such as `find the most efficient means to your ends.' Reason itself does not generate the demand that our ends accord with the Categorical Imperative. It is the richer concept of free-will which implies moral obligation.

The Metaphysics of Freedom

Kant's deduction of morality is not yet complete. He has not proved that morality is not an illusion or "phantom of the brain". The argument so far has shown that if we are beings with a free-will, then the Categorical Imperative applies to us. But Kant has not yet argued for the claim that we are free beings. The claim is problematic because the notion of a free will is that of something unconditioned. However, every event in the phenomenal world is caused. Therefore, even our own actions are causally determined. Yet, Kant insists we must view our actions as free. How can he justify the second premise (of argument

A above) - that we are free? First, Kant's solution to the problem of how freedom is possible given causality. As we saw in the discussion of the Third Antinomy, it is to affirm that we can regard ourselves in two ways. As a part of the natural or phenomenal world, our actions are causally determined. As noumenal beings, who do not belong to the spatio-temporal phenomenal world, we can regard ourselves as free. In this way, Kant tries to reconcile determinism and freedom.

In the third chapter of the Groundwork, Kant is careful not to claim that we know ourselves to be beings with a free-will. We cannot assert such propositional or theoretical knowledge because Freedom is an Idea of Reason which nothing in the natural world can correspond to. Knowledge is confined to the objects of possible experience. For these reasons, in the Groundwork, Kant does not argue for premise 2 as it stands. Instead he argues that theoretical metaphysics does not preclude us thinking of noumenal freedom as something possible.

The *Critique of Practical Reason* adopts a very different approach. As we have seen, in the *Groundwork* Kant tries to deduce morality from freedom. This approach suffers from the limitation that we cannot know that we are free; freedom has to be presupposed. In the second Critique Kant tries to show that the claim that we are free can be justified on moral grounds (i.e. that the idea of freedom can be justified because it is a requirement of morality).

This new approach allows Kant to argue that morality transforms the otherwise empty noumenal idea of the unconditioned will. As we have seen, in the first Critique, the categories have no real content beyond possible experience, and therefore the idea of noumena is empty. But now Kant argues that noumenal ideas may have a different kind of content, in relation to the practical or morality. For instance, the idea of the will necessarily acquires meaning in relation to the moral. The vacant hole left by theory is filled by practice.

Virtue Theory

The *Groundwork* is primarily an attempt to identify and justify the a priori element in morality. The *Metaphysic of Morals* gives us a less formal and abstract characterization of morality. It is divided into two parts: the metaphysical elements of law, and the metaphysical elements of virtue. This division reflects Kant's distinction between juridical and ethical duties. Juridical duties concern the external aspect of action and correspond to moral rights. If I act unjustly towards someone then I infringe their rights. Ethical duties, on the other hand, concern the motivation of action and do not correspond to moral rights. For example, I have ethical duty to help other people, but this does not mean that they have a right to this help, according to Kant. In this section we shall concentrate on Kant's doctrine of virtue.

According to Kant, the Categorical Imperative makes certain ends obligations for our will. These are ones own perfection and the happiness of others. This cannot be reversed to ones own happiness and the perfection of others! First this is because ones own instincts lead one to seek happiness for oneself and therefore it is not a duty; and second, because it is not in ones power to change the ends of another.

Kant divides perfection into two elements: natural and moral. Natural perfection consists in cultivating ones powers, such as reasoning, imagination, health and other talents. Clearly the Categorical Imperative does not enjoin one to do this for the sake of some advantage. It enjoins us to seek perfection, because the power to set ones own ends is a defining characteristic of humanity. Because of this we have the duty to make ourselves worthy of humanity.

Some Problems

The metaphysics of Kant's moral theory leaves us with three problems. The first is whether Kant's attitude to the concept of noumena in his ethical work is really compatible with that of the first Critique. A consistent reading of the first Critique requires a weak interpretation of Transcendental Idealism, according to which he is not asserting the existence of two realms, but rather stressing the non-absolute nature of empirical reality. At times it seems his moral theory might require a stronger interpretation of Transcendental Idealism.

The second problem is whether moral evil or badness is really possible give his account. At the beginning of the third chapter of the Groundwork, Kant seems to claim free-will shall necessarily conform to the moral law. This would mean that only unfree actions can be morally bad. Kant addresses his problem in *the Religion within the Bounds of Reason Alone* by distinguishing *Wille*, the will and *Wilkür*, the power of choice. He argues that the *Wille* is identical to practical reason and it is not free or unfree. The *Wilkür* must freely decide whether to follow the dictates of reason or the promptings of desire.

The third problem is whether we as phenomenal beings can even make sense of the moral imperative given that it is noumenal. Kant was aware of this problem and tries to solve it in the Third Critique - the Critique of Judgment, which is the theme of the last chapter.

9
Politics

Karl Marx called Kant *the* political philosopher of the French Revolution. Marx's early view of work in the 1844 manuscripts is in part Kantian inspired: capitalism requires that the laborer treat his work merely as a means and this results in alienation. On a more conservative and homely note, Kant's political philosophy captures the spirit of the American revolution, because the core of his moral philosophy is the freedom of the individual.

For Kant, politics is a practical application of the Categorical Imperative. Politics is not merely a question of Machievellian expediency, or of egoistic power struggles. His political theory is based on the moral ideal of individual autonomy. The function and justification of the state is to preserve that individual autonomy. Kant's political theory is largely contained in the second part of the *Metaphysics of Morals* (1797): the doctrine of law.

To apply the Categorical Imperative to the management of civil society requires the law. Politics is concerned with the just resolution of conflicts of interest. This requires criteria which will be universal, which Kant thinks of as the law. Politics requires law.

Despite its necessary connection to morality, the doctrine of law is different from the doctrine of virtue. Morality, as a form of virtue, makes demands on our will and inner motivation. The law makes demands on our external action, not on our motivation. According to Kant, as a consequence of this difference, political duties are always perfect duties towards others. They are not duties to oneself and politics

72

does not include imperfect duties to others, such as acts of benevolence. The purpose of politics should not be to make people happy and benevolent despotism cannot be justified on such grounds. Therefore, we can say that law is concerned with the outer, and enforceable aspect of perfect moral duties to others.

The universal principle of right is concerned with the a priori form of politics, rather than the empirical specifics. This form is the reconciliation of each person's freedom with that of the others in accordance with a universal law. The political ideal of right is when the will of one person can be unified with the will of another under a universal law of freedom. Kant's idea is that it is a condition of external freedom that there be an enforced law. Freedom requires some coercion. In other words, freedom implies that it is morally legitimate to use coercion, on the basis of the law, against someone who infringes the freedom of others. Any other type of coercion is wrong.

For this principle of right to be applied by a state requires a "constitution allowing the greatest possible human freedom in accordance with laws which ensure the freedom of each can coexist with the freedom of all the others." This is the fundamental principle of politics.

The state is a group united under a common law. But, as rational beings, we must treat ourselves as ends and as autonomous law givers. Consequently, all societal laws must be ones which the people would agree to, and all laws must be made public. Anything else would contradict our autonomous nature. For this reason, the state should be justified in terms of an original social contract. However, Kant gives this idea a novel twist.

He does not think of the social contract as a historical fact, as Rousseau tends to, but rather as a practical Idea of Reason. According to this, for external matters, people should be willing to submit their individual will to the universal Will. The universal will does not mean the will of the majority (as does Rousseau by "general will"). For Kant it means an Idea of reason, which justifies government by law.

The problem of many social contract theories is that they are stuck in a dilemma. On the one hand, if there really had been a binding social contract, then it might justify the state. However, we know that the idea of a social contract is a historical fiction. On the other hand, the idea of a purely hypothetical social contract, one that could have been made but never was, does seem to justify anything (one is not bound by a promise that one never made). Kant escapes this dilemma by taking the idea of a social contract as a moral ideal inherent in universal reason. It is what we all ought to agree to. It is a norm. In practice this norm implies that the legislator should apply the test of universalizability to the laws in question.

This interpretation of social contract allows Kant to give a novel justification of the right to private property. It is a postulate of practical reason that it be possible in principle for anyone to own any piece of property and thereby exclude others from the use of it. In other words, private property is a fundamental right. Kant does not justify this right pragmatically, or in terms of its usefulness. He thinks that this right derives from the a priori right to freedom; property is the external guarantee of freedom.

Philosophically, the right to property is problematic because of the difficulties in justifying the original act of appropriation. Someone claims a piece of previously unowned land as "mine." Kant tries to justify such appropriations in terms of the social contract. Property makes the establishment of the system of law and the state necessary. In other words, we ought to have authorized such original acts of appropriation because it is right to have a state (i.e. to make institutional legislation for the protection of rights). The need for a state justifies private property, rather than the other way around. This argument departs radically from John Locke's attempt to justify appropriation empirically in terms of labor.

According to Kant, the establishment of a state is not a question of prudence or greater utility, but is a requirement of reason or the Categorical Imperative itself. The right to freedom of each should be protected by a system of universal law according to the social contract. The Idea of the social contract requires a constitution for establishing the state, and this in turn should specify a separation of powers. In these terms, Kant defines a republican form of government. It requires the distinction between legislature, executive and judiciary. In making this separation, Kant is not arguing against all monarchies. He does, however, claim that sovereign authority should reside with the people and that this could be through a legislative representative assembly.

Kant's claim about the supremacy of law apparently makes rebellion and revolution morally wrong, because such actions violate the constitution, and break the social contract. Even if a constitution had a clause permitting rebellion in exceptional circumstances, there could be no authority to judge the application of that clause. Such a person or body would amount to a second sovereign, which would be a contradiction. However, the citizens must have a right to make public and open criticism of the government, and this right would be guaranteed by a republican constitution. However, for Kant, free speech is not an overriding right. Just as we cannot be free to destroy freedom, we should not tolerate speech which destroys tolerance. In other words, the right to public criticism does not extend to violating the constitution which protects that right. According to Kant, laws which permit breaking the constitution cannot be universalized consistently. They deny their own presupposition.

From the fundamental principle of politics, Kant derives three further principles. The first is freedom. Political freedom requires laws; so these should be seen as conditions for freedom, and not as limitations or coercions. Political freedom is independence from the coercion of the will of another person. In a civil society, the law should not be the will of any person, but should something which everyone can assent to. The law should be universal in this sense. The right to freedom therefore is incompatible with political paternalism. The second is equality before the law. There can be no exceptions or privileges in the law, for it is universal. Note that Kant's notion of equality is purely procedural and contains no idea of economic equality. The third is self-dependence, or self sufficiency. which is requirement of the right to vote.

For Kant the ultimate aim of politics is to achieve a just order of perpetual peace. This ideal requires extending the ideals of politics to the international. Kant thinks that a peaceful confederation of republics is the best possibility for this ideal. For Kant, the political ideal is not attainable but we can approach it. Indeed, Kant thinks that to understand history, we must assume that there is a purpose or plan in the unfolding of events. Kant does not mean that there is such a plan, but only that without the Idea, history cannot be understood. Since the nature of persons is free-will, we should assume that the plan of nature is our education towards a state of freedom and rationality. History is a process towards greater freedom, but this does not mean that all change is progress. This historical process involves humankind as a whole. It is our story.

10

God and Religion

It seems that Kant has an ambivalent attitude towards the supersensible or noumena. On the one hand, in the *Critique of Pure Reason*, he argues forcefully against the Rationalist assumption that we can have theoretical knowledge of noumena, by insisting that the categories only have meaning in relation to possible experience. On the other hand, especially in the *Critique of Practical Reason*, he apparently defends some of the metaphysical claims of religion arguing that they are presupposed by morality. Superficially, it seems that Kant both wants to deny and affirm the supersensible or noumenal. This tension makes his philosophy more interesting; an outright rejection or acceptance of the supersensible might appear crudely one sided. However, we need to state his position carefully to avoid contradiction.

This same conflict appears in Kant's discussion of God and religion. In part the answer to this conflict is to see how his views on God and religion are part of his moral philosophy. For Kant, morality does not depend on religion, religion depends on morality. The basis and justification of religious conviction is our moral feeling or the moral law. In the end, morality requires us to have faith in God (or at least that God is possible). Any claim to (theoretical) knowledge of God's existence is utterly mistaken. Of course, viewing Kant's views on religion as an outgrowth of his theory of morals still leaves us with the general question of how to reconcile the first and second critiques. Kant's views on nature and morality seem at odds with each other. This reconciliation does not take place until the Third Critique.

Kant's ambivalence towards metaphysics makes him an interesting religious thinker, at odds with the church. At times, especially to the orthodox, Kant's moral based theology looks almost like agnosticism. His view of morals conflicts with some traditional Christian ceremonial practices. In brief, for Kant, the worship of God and religious practice really should consist in respecting morality. Anything beyond that would be superstition or a denial of inner freedom. Effectively for Kant, to worship God is to act morally for this itself is a recognition of holiness; "Everything apart from a moral way of life, man believe himself capable of doing to please God is mere religious delusion." After the publication of *Religion within the Bounds of Reason Alone* (1793), king Wilheim II wrote to Kant to forbid him from publishing more on religion. Kant obeyed until the king's death in 1797.

Against the Proofs

For Kant, the idea of God is an idea of Reason. Like all the ideas of Reason, it cannot be exhibited in experience. God is not an object of possible experience and, therefore, God cannot be a part of the natural world. So Kant claims that it is impossible to show that God exists. But he also says we can have the idea of such a being as a noumenon, although such a thought can never amount to knowledge. In this way, Kant's views on God have two sides: one, an attack on the traditional proofs of God's existence and two, an explanation of our idea of God.

Kant claims that all proofs of God's existence can be reduced to three arguments: the ontological argument, the cosmological argument and the physico-theological argument. He attacks the ontological argument on the grounds that existence is not a predicate or property (A 626). He says that existence is merely the copula of a judgment. The proposition 'God is perfect' contains only two concepts, `God' and `perfect'; the small word `is' adds no new predicate. In other words, there is no difference between the idea of a God who exists and the idea of a God who does not exist. Existence adds nothing to the idea of God, and so existence cannot be a perfection (contrary to what is claimed in the ontological argument). Kant also says that all existential propositions are synthetic and argues against the idea of necessary existence. At A 622-3 he says that even if God is an absolutely necessary being, this does not mean that God necessarily exists. It only means that if God exists then a necessary being exists. It is compatible with this to deny that God exists.

The cosmological proof of God's existence is as follows. If

anything contingent exists, then something necessary must exist. Since something contingent does exist, so does the necessary, and this must be God. Kant concentrates on the last part of this argument, that is on the move from `something necessary exists' to `God exists.' He claims that this step of the argument presupposes the ontological argument. The assertion that nothing could be a necessary being but God involves the assertion that if anything is a necessary being then it is God and the assertion that if anything is God then it is a necessary being. Kant claims that this second assertion involves the ontological argument.

The physico-theological argument is often called `the argument from design.' Kant says that the order in nature does not show the need for a creator nor the need for a designer. According to Kant, the argument from design presupposes the cosmological argument, because the argument from design moves from the existence of order in nature to the existence of a necessary being, and hence God. Having rejected the cosmological, the ontological argument and the notion of necessary existence, Kant can reject the argument from design.

The Idea of God

Kant claims that the idea of God, like that of freedom, is the idea of the unconditioned. The unconditioned can never be met with in experience and, therefore, it is not an object in the phenomenal world. To think of God as a substance or object is a mistake. It is equivalent to affirming Transcendental Realism, or asserting the positive concept of a noumena. In this way, Reason cannot give us metaphysical a priori knowledge of an absolute reality.

Kant is not merely denying the possibility of knowledge. His criticism is more radical; he is denying meaning. The function and meaning of the categories is in relation to possible experience. Apart from that role, they have no sense; they are empty (B707). This is why we have no positive notion of noumena. Kant is prescribing the bounds of sense, in both senses of `sense'. Therefore, God is an empty limiting concept, the wrong side of this boundary. This is part of the diagnosis of the error of Pure Reason.

Despite this error, the ideas of the unconditioned are an inevitable part of Reason because Reason seeks a complete explanation. They are essential to the way Reason functions. The mistake is to think that the world will conform to these Ideas. The error is to not realize that these Ideas are merely regulative and not constitutive. The Idea of God stands as an ideal of Reason which can never be met in the empirical world.

Kant explains the specific Idea of God in terms of an unconditioned Idea of the total reality. Any particular thing is determinate with respect to all pairs of contradictory predicates; either it is red or not red, round or not... This principle (that all existing things are completely determinate) requires the idea of all possible predicates (A572), as opposed to the predicates we know. It requires the unconditioned idea of a complete totality or the sum of all reality. This unconditioned idea leads to the ideal of a thing containing all of realities, which Kant calls the *ens realissimum*. This ideal is our concept of God, the only really complete thing (A576).

In the Lectures on Philosophical Theology, Kant draws an interesting distinction between deism and theism. A deist believes in God but as "an eternal nature at the root of all things." The deist believes in an impersonal God. The theist believes in God as a moral, living being. Such a conception borrows features from everyday life by analogy. For example, we represent the idea of God as a will on analogy with our own will.

A Practical Vindication

Kant says that he abolishes knowledge to make room for faith (Bxxx). It might be more accurate to say that he abolishes theoretical knowledge to make room for practical knowledge. Faith is not merely unsupported opinion (A820). Kant thinks that there are arguments based on morality which make belief in God rationally required.

In the *Critique of Practical Reason*, Kant argues because we are bound by the moral law, we must view ourselves as free. Yet we cannot know that we are free. Although a person must regard themselves as a human being in the natural world, governed by causal laws, at the same time, it is a requirement of morality and action, that we also regard ourselves also as noumenal beings free from these laws. This is called the first postulate of practical reason.

Kant thinks that the immortality of the soul and the idea of God are similar but indirect requirements of morality (which are the second and third postulates). To understand why, we must look at his notion of the *summum bonum* or the perfect good. Reason seeks an unconditioned totality. In its theoretical function, this unconditioned is expressed as the Ideas of Reason (see Ch. 7). In its practical function, the object of Reason is the perfect good. This is the ideal at which practical reason aims. Obviously, according to Kant, this is defined in terms of virtue or the good will. However, although the good will is good without qualification, it is more perfect when it brings happiness. The perfect good contains two elements virtue and happiness.

According to Kant, the connection between virtue and happiness is not analytic. The one idea is not contained in the other; the connection is synthetic. However, it is not empirical, because virtue does not always bring happiness and happy people are not always virtuous. The connection is that virtue ideally ought to cause happiness and this is expressed by a practical synthetic a priori claim. It is not a theoretical synthetic a priori truth - it is not a necessary condition of experience. Certainly Kant is not claiming that we should will in the morally right way because, in the long run, this shall make us happy. Such a claim would contradict the fundamentals of his moral philosophy by making morality heteronomous. Although justice requires that virtue should bring happiness, morality requires virtue, but not for the sake of happiness. Virtue is for its own sake.

The *summum bonum* or the perfect good is the ideal of practical reason. Therefore, insofar as we are noumenal beings with a free will, we must believe that this ideal is attainable. From this point, Kant derives the ideas of immortality and God. Immortality is a practical precondition for the ideal of perfect virtue. We must think that the ideal of the perfect good is attainable. The core of this ideal is perfect virtue, according to which a person's will is in complete accord with the moral law. Kant defines this as holiness, because God's will must be perfect in this way. Of course, us humans, as beings who live in the natural world, cannot achieve this holiness in our life time. The ideal presents itself to us as an endless task of progressing towards the ideal. The ideal, therefore, requires immortality - "the unending duration of the existence and personality of the same rational being." (220) In stark contrast, remember the Paralogisms of the first Critique. Kant argues against Descartes that the immortality of the soul cannot be asserted, because it mistakes the unity of consciousness for the consciousness of a unity. Descartes illegitimately takes the `I think' to be a permanent substance.

Kant thinks the two Critiques can be reconciled because in the second Critique he is not asserting that we can know we are immortal. From the standpoint of theoretical knowledge, immortality cannot be asserted; knowledge is necessarily confined to the phenomenal world of things in space and time. However, from the standpoint of morality, immortality must be postulated. To deny it is equivalent to claiming that the ideal of perfect virtue or holiness is unattainable which is equivalent to denying it as an ideal, which in turn is a rejection of morality. Kant effects his reconciliation by denying the possibility of theoretical knowledge but affirming the necessity of practical knowledge.

The third postulate of practical reason is God. In effect, God guarantees the synthetic and a priori connection between virtue and happiness. God as an all good being is required for the idea that happiness should be proportioned according to virtue, as justice requires. This does not consist a proof of the existence of God. It is rather an argument to show us that belief in God is inherent in our moral understanding and practice. Belief that the moral ideal of the *summum bonum* is attainable implicitly requires belief in God. Therefore, pursuit of the highest good justifies belief in God.

This does not mean that morality depends on God. Kant says:

> Morality in so far as it is grounded in the concept of man as a being who is free... needs neither the idea of another being above man for the latter to recognize his duty, nor any other motive than the law itself.

Also, it does not mean that we can affirm that God exists. The second and third postulates of practical reason do not amount to a theoretical defense of an immortal soul and of a just God. Kant calls a postulate a "practically necessary hypothesis." (11-12) This means even though there are no have grounds for asserting that God exits, we have moral reasons to view the universe and act as though He does. If we do not view the universe and ourselves in this way, then we will involved in an inconsistency or irrationality with regard to morality. The two postulates are presupposed if the ideals of morality are realizable, which, according to Kant, they must be if we ought to strive for them.

Despite these clarifications, it seems difficult to reconcile Kant's criticisms of Rationalism in the first Critique with the moral theology of the second Critique. In part this is because Kant sometimes writes as if the moral argument gives evidence for the reality of God. This is something he should not say. This, however, is a minor inconsistency and not a worrying problem. The more profound problem is that in the first Critique Kant affirms that the notion of a noumena is only an empty limiting concept and that we cannot meaningfully apply the categories beyond the realm of possible experience. Therefore, Kant's point is not so much the knowledge claim that we lack evidence for the existence of God, but rather the meaning claim that such talk has no real meaning because it involves using the categories beyond the bounds of sense. As we have seen, this problem does not only affect Kant's view of God, it also haunts his conception of Freedom and his moral philosophy. Fortunately, Kant recognizes the problem, and in the Third Critique he tries to solve it.

11

The Beauty of Teleology

The Introduction to the *Critique of Judgment* sets out a pressing problem inherited from the earlier two Critiques: the phenomenal and noumenal are like two separate worlds. Kant says:

> The concept of freedom determines nothing in respect of the
> theoretical cognition of nature; and the concept of nature
> likewise nothing in respect of the practical laws of freedom.
> (M, p.37)

If there is an unbridgeable gap between the two realms, then how can Kant's moral philosophy be relevant to the natural world? How can the natural world be a proper medium for moral ends?

Kant seeks the solution in the nature of judgment. We understand nature by positing general principles and classifications which explain natural phenomena, or, in Kant's terminology, reflective judgment aims to discover universals which apply to particulars. According to Kant, in ascending from the particular to the universal, judgment needs to assume a priori that nature is understandable for beings like us (for example that causal laws can be explained by a small number of more general causal principles).

This a priori assumption of judgment does not determine how the world actually is, but only how we should view it. We should view the world as comprehensible for finite minds like ours. In effect, we should regard nature as if it were a superhuman work of art, the product of a creative understanding seeking to render everything comprehensible for us. Kant says

> Particular causal laws must be regarded...according to a unity such as there would have been if an understanding had supplied them for the benefit of our cognitive faculties. (M., p.19)

When the world accords with this self-imposed view, we feel aesthetic pleasure and this feeling governs the beautiful.

How does this relate to Kant's aim of linking the first two Critiques? The a priori principle of judgment enables us to think that nature is not entirely alien to the realization of moral ends. Beauty allows us to regard nature as if it were a phenomenal manifestation of the noumenal and it leads us to consider nature as a giant work of art expressing the supersensible. This gives us reason to believe, or at least hope, that noumenal moral concepts can have a phenomenal realization.

Beauty

According to Kant, aesthetic delight is unique amongst pleasures because it is disinterested. A beautiful object arouses our delight without appeal to our desires or will. Hence, the subject cannot find the ground of this pleasure in any idiosyncratic desires. Furthermore, aesthetic pleasure must be grounded in something common to every person, and consequently the subject must believe that he or she has a reason for attributing a similar aesthetic pleasure to everyone. From this Kant concludes that we demand universal and necessary agreement from others concerning what is beautiful. If I judge something to be beautiful, I implicitly claim that others ought to find it so too (and that if they do not that they are in some sense mistaken). For this reason, Kant says that it is as if aesthetic judgments were objective.

What makes a natural object beautiful? Kant's answer has three levels to it. The first is negative: Kant denies that we can answer this question by appealing to any determinate concept or set of rules that lay down when an object is beautiful. Despite his claim that aesthetic judgments demand universal agreement, Kant denies that they are strictly objective. To judge that an object is beautiful, I must rely on my own feelings rather than on any rules or determinate concepts. This means that we cannot settle aesthetic disputes nor specify what is beautiful about an object by referring to any rules .

Second, Kant's positive answer is based on judgment's a priori assumption that nature is understandable. An object is beautiful when our perception of it leads us to feel justified in regarding nature as comprehensible. This consists in viewing nature as if it had been created by an intelligence other than ours for that very purpose, so that our understanding feels at home. A beautiful object makes us feel justified in regarding nature as though it were created for a purpose, although no specific purpose of ours is involved in aesthetic judgments. In other words, the beautiful encapsulates purposefulness without any actual purpose.

Third, Kant adds a psychological slant to his teleological answer. When we perceive something beautiful, our faculties synthesize the raw data of perception in an especially smooth and harmonious fashion. Aesthetic pleasure is based on the harmonious functioning of the faculties. We perceive a beautiful rose as something perfect or just right because we feel as if its form or shape embodies some purpose and this results in the disinterested pleasure of beauty.

The reconciliation

Kant's theory of beauty links the first and second Critiques. The separation of the theoretical and moral is necessary to make both possible: the natural world is causally determined; morality requires freedom. However, Kant must deny that the moral prescriptions only apply to the noumenal will. Such a claim would effectively render the moral law irrelevant to the mechanical Newtonian world in which we perform our everyday actions. But, how can a noumenally prescribed moral law be applicable to feelings and actions occurring in a causally mechanical world?

The main problem is a question of how the phenomenal can have moral content. Unlike concepts, ideas do not have instances; if concepts without intuitions are empty, ideas without instances must be hollow. The problem of the Third Critique is 'How can the noumenal idea of freedom have content (i.e. be more than an empty limiting idea) for phenomenal beings?' The issue is: 'How is it possible for a supersensible moral law to apply meaningfully to the natural world? ' or 'How is phenomenalised morality possible?'

The solution is an essentially simple idea: judgment has to make certain assumptions about nature for scientific investigation to be possible. Quite independently, that same assumption is required for phenomenalised morality to be possible. When the world appears to accord with judgments assumption we feel beauty. In other words, beauty is the feeling that the world conforms to judgment's assumption and thereby we regard nature as though it has a purpose. And this condition gives us the hope that phenomenalised morality is possible.

Kant's characterization of the principle of judgment has two elements. The first represents nature as being understandable for us, for example, because of the unity of empirical causal laws; the second is shaped by the quasi- teleological: the idea that we must regard nature as if it were designed.

In attempting to understand the world, we should adopt the general working assumption that nature is understandable. This first interpretation of the principle states a goal or standard for reflective judgment, although the judgments we actually make may not conform to the standard. When we are judging well for example, we might use the idea of the simplicity of nature to guide our investigations. Without such a standard we can have no hope of gaining systematic empirical knowledge. The principle thus sets a goal which is functionally necessary for certain tasks. As it is only a heuristic guide, we do not pretend that nature must conform to that standard.

From this general assumption more exact hypotheses can be derived. These hypotheses make specific predictions or claims about nature which can be confirmed or falsified, even though the general principle itself cannot. When the specific predictions appear to be falsified through observation, we should not therefore abandon the general principle, but rather continue our inquiry hoping to reveal a unity or simplicity in nature at a deeper level than we have thus far been investigating. Because the general principle makes a claim about what we can do (i.e. we can unify the multifarious empirical laws of physics), it can't be definitely falsified: there could always be more evidence waiting around the experimental corner.

The second element of judgment's a priori principle is teleological: the idea of the formal finality of nature. Kant often says we must regard nature as if it were designed. This is more than a functional working assumption or guide for specific tasks; it is a perceptual viewpoint projected onto the world. It tells us that we must regard nature as though it were designed and were a giant work of art expressing the supersensible. Regarding nature as final is not merely like employing a working hypothesis as an investigative guide; it is more like being influenced by a mood which taints and transforms ones perceptions. However, there may be no first order perceptual difference between viewing nature as designed and viewing it as a mechanical system. In holding a quasi-teleological view of nature, one does not attribute any specific properties to the world. Finality is not a property of nature.

Judgment's assumption is a priori in that it is not acquired through experience; its source is judgment itself. However it is not a priori in the sense of being a necessary condition of experience and consequently does not define the form of the natural world. Kant also denies that it is merely psychologically necessary; instead of describing how we actually do judge or view nature, it indicates how we ought to do so. What does 'ought' mean here ? How is judgment's principle justified as a standard ? If one were asked to justify the first version of the principle in its general form, a reasonable response would be: "without using some such working hypothesis I cannot continue scientific investigation systematically; I must assume that nature is understandable, even if many specific areas of investigation seem incomprehensible. Even if I am surrounded by a multitude of apparently disparate facts, to assume that nature is not in the final analysis understandable is to give up the investigation, or to capitulate at the moment of incomprehension." In other words it is a necessary condition of gaining systematic empirical knowledge. Furthermore, to assume that nature is incomprehensible would be to surrender the idea of rational inquiry.

Kant maintains that the transition between the phenomenal and noumenal is made possible by the idea of finality. How does it do that ? If we view the world through the eyes of finality, we shall regard it as amenable to the phenomenalisation of morality and also as beautiful. As explained earlier, Kant thinks we ought to regard nature in this way. Because the feeling of beauty gives us the hope that morality can be phenomenalized, we have a moral interest in the beauty of the world. This does not mean that beauty is reducible to morality. Kant insists that aesthetics is autonomous from morality.

As well as saying that we have a moral interest in the beautiful, Kant claims that beauty symbolizes the morally good. Beauty is requires the idea of the form of purposefulness. This idea of form requires the idea of a noumenal will. The beautiful is a symbol of the good because the concept of beauty requires the hypothetical supposition of a noumenal will which designs nature in order to make it understandable for creatures cognitively constituted like us. Because a will should be considered morally good, natural beauty symbolizes the good by analogy with it.

One of the interesting features of Kant's aesthetic theory is his analysis of the objectivity of beauty. Beauty is a feeling which arises in the beholder, and therefore, it is not an objective property of things. However, Kant claims about that judgments about what is beautiful can be mistaken; we ought to agree about what is beautiful. At the same time, he also claims that there are no rules to which we can appeal to spell out when a thing ought to be judged beautiful.

The Sublime

Kant also analyses another kind of aesthetic pleasure, the sublime, which is afforded by contemplating the noumenal Ideas of Reason. Whereas only the Ideas of Reason may be strictly called sublime, things in nature which lead to the contemplation of these Ideas may be regarded as sublime in a derivative sense. When nature does violence to our faculties, the mind is enticed away from the sensible world towards the supersensible Ideas of Reason within, and this causes us pleasure. When nature is wild, irregular, powerful and mighty and seems to run counter to our faculties, it is initially repellent to the mind. However, at the same time, we have a heightened awareness of the inadequacy of the sensible world in representing the Ideas, which we are then led to contemplate with disinterested pleasure.

There are important differences between the beautiful and the sublime: with the beautiful we find finality in nature; with the sublime we find it in the supersensible Ideas of Reason. Yet these two aesthetic feelings have much in common. Both are pleasing on their own account, and in neither case does the delight depend upon our interests or upon any definite concept. Furthermore, both kinds of judgment are subjective and yet universally valid, although in the case of sublimity Kant says that universal and necessary agreement can only be demanded through the moral law:

> The pleasure in the sublime in nature ... lays claim also to
> universal participation, but still it presupposes another feeling
> that, namely of our supersensible sphere which... has a moral
> foundation... We may still demand that delight from everyone;
> but we can do so only through the moral law. (M. p.149)

Teleology

The *Critique of Judgment* has two parts. The first explains how
beauty is possible because of the form of purpose and as such is
concerned with formal teleological judgment, The second part is
concerned with purpose in nature,or material teleological judgments.
The idea which unifies them is that we need to regard nature as more
than a mechanical system in order to use the idea of freedom. We need
to think of nature itself in its totality as a presentation of something
supersensible.

Kant notes that we sometimes attribute external purposes to things
in nature. For example, we say that the grass exists for the reindeer to
eat, and the reindeer for the humans who hunt them. However, Kant
raises this possibility only to discard it. He is sceptical of judgments of
external purposes in nature. He argues that it is impossible for any such
judgments to be justified. (Therefore one would have equal
justification is claiming that humans exist for the sake of maggots). He
says that a better explanation is that cows are able to live where there is
grass, and humans hunt in the north because there are reindeer there.

However, Kant distinguishes these external purposes from internal
ones. Internal purpose belongs to things in nature which embody
purpose. Instead of having a purpose in relation to something external,
they are a purpose. For example, consider the growth of a tree. The tree
organizes matter in a process of self-production and this process
depends on a mutual dependency of whole and part - the tree as a whole
needs the leaves which it itself produces. Kant says that something has
its own internal purpose when it is cause and effect of itself in two
ways. First, in a purposive whole, "each part exists by means of all the
other parts and is regarded as existing for the sake of the whole." (286).
Of course, this is not sufficient to distinguish an organic whole from an
artifact like a watch. This is why Kant adds the second condition: the
being must be self organizing, in the sense that the parts must be
regarded as reciprocally producing each other. Such a self-organizing
whole has what Kant calls formative power.

With these two points in hand, Kant gives a definition of internal purposiveness: "An organized product of nature is one in which everything is reciprocally end and means." He thinks that this serves to define "organism" and that this Idea of the ends of nature is a necessary guiding principle in our scientific study. Scientists who "dissect plants and animals" seek to investigate their structure and "see into the reasons why ..the parts have such and such a position." (376). Kant thinks of this principle as an a priori regulative Idea of judgment for interpreting nature. It is not empirical, but neither is it a necessary condition of experience.

Kant claims that this principle requires us to regard nature as governed by more than by blind causal mechanisms. He does not mean that we have to postulate hidden supersensible causes, in addition to the natural causes, for that would contradict the letter and spirit of the first Critique. He means that mechanical causes in nature have to be viewed also teleologically (377).

On the one hand, Kant is sceptical concerning external purposes. He also thinks that the Idea of internal purpose can be applied only to self-organizing beings and not to inorganic things. On the other hand, Kant thinks that the Idea of Finality can be extended to interpreting nature as a system of ends. Using it as a regulative principle, we can unify the whole of Nature as a system through this Idea. Indeed, we can view it analogous to a vast single organism.

This, however, Kant assures us does not mean that we are justified in asserting that Nature really does have a purpose. The Idea of purpose is only a regulative principle of reflective judgment. Furthermore, Kant points out that the idea of the purpose of Nature requires the Idea of a supersensible God, an intelligent cause of Nature. However, the regulative Idea of judgment gives us no reason to affirm the existence of God.

Are mechanical laws on their own sufficient to explain natural phenomena? The first maxim of judgment says that they are. On the other hand, organic beings are characterized using the Idea of internal purpose. This means that mere mechanical causality is not sufficient to judge them. The second maxim of judgment says that some things in Nature are not possible merely due to mechanical causation.

Kant calls this apparent contradiction the antinomy of teleological judgment. He resolves it by denying that there really is a contradiction. The two maxims of judgment are principles of investigation and not constitutive of the phenomenal world.

12
Conclusion

How can the scientific world view be reconciled with the claims of morality and religion? The standard interpretation makes Kant's answer very similar to Descartes' dualism. There are two worlds, the noumenal and the phenomenal. One main difference is that in Kant the two worlds cannot intereact. Another is that in Kant, the noumenal is both non-spatial and non -temporal. These points make Kant's two world answer less appealing than even Descartes'. Furthermore, Kant cannot consistently maintain the two world theory; it contradicts major claims of the first Critique. Despite this, there is much textual evidence to support this two world reading.

There is another way to understand Kant's answer, which also has some textual support. There is only one world. It is this causally determined world of things in space and time. Yet, we are compelled to view this world, and more importantly, ourselves and our actions, in another way: in accordance with the idea of Freedom. How is possible? Kant's answer has thee layers.

First, the negative notion of noumena is implied by the scientific world view. This is because Empiricism does not work in explaining knowledge. It cannot account for the structural features of the natural world and experience itself. It cannot account for the synthetic a priori. The synthetic a priori shows that the negative notion of noumena is necessary, not as additional thing, but as a limit on our knowledge.

Second, our moral experience requires the notion of noumena. We can never know that we are free, but freedom, and therefore reason are presuppositions of morality. In this sense, the ideas and ideals of reason acquire a meaning in relation to practice, even though they cannot extend our knowledge of the world. In this way too, we can make sense of some of the claims of religion. In order for morality to make sense, we must regard ourselves as noumenal wills.

So far, we have not implied the existence of two worlds. However, Kant's position is not yet complete: morality and freedom are not yet fully reconciled with the scientific view. Are we justified in viewing ourselves in this other way? We can justify viewing ourselves as noumena by appealing to the categorical nature of morality. Morality requires freedom. Also, we can show that morality is not an illusion by appealing to the claim that we are free agents. Freedom implies morality. These two points show us that freedom and morality stand or fall together. However, the problem still remains. The first Critique affirms that, as beings in the natural world, we can have no empirical evidence that the claims of morality really are applicable to us. The Idea of the unconditioned will is not an object of experience, nor is it a necessary condition of experience. Therefore, it seems that there can be no reason for thinking that moral claims apply to us as natural beings.

Kant's third point is that the practice of science requires us to view nature as a teleological system of ends. We have no option but to regard the causal mechanisms of nature as if they worked for a purpose. Otherwise, there would be no possibility of understanding organisms. Furthermore, the feeling of beauty gives us the hope that the universe is our home and suitable for the realization of a moral life. In other words, this feeling gives us the sense that we are not mistaken in viewing nature as the expression of something absolute. Not that there are two worlds - rather than we are right in thinking that this world (which we necessarily view mechanically) should be viewed also non mechanically, as a system of ends.

The answer then amounts to the following: we are compelled to view this world as more than mechanical for reasons quite apart from morality. This "justifies" or "supports" our viewing ourselves and actions in the same way.

To work this answer needs to satisfy two conditions. First, it requires that Kant is not asserting that there are two worlds, the phenomenal and noumenal, but rather that there are two ways to regard the one world. Second it requires that we can make sense of the notion of justification by appeal to practice and feeling used by Kant.

BIBLIOGRAPHY

Allison, Henry, *Kant's Transcendental Idealism*, Yale, 1983

Allison, Henry, *Kant's Theory of Freedom*, Cambridge, 1990

Aune, Bruce, *Kant's Theory of Morals*, Princenton, 1979

Bennett, *Kant's Analytic*, Cambridge, 1966

Bennett, *Kant's Dialectic*, Cambridge, 1974

Brittain, Gordon , *Kant's Theory of Science*, Princeton University
Press, 1975

Cassirer, Ernst, *Kant's Life and Thought*, Yale, 1981

Cohen Ted and Guyer, Paul eds, *Essays in Kant's Aesthetics*, The
University of Chicago Press, 1982

Forster, Eckhart, ed., *Kant's Transcendental Deductions: the Three
"Critiques" and the "Opus Postumum"*, Stanford, 1989

Guyer, Paul, *Kant and the Claims of Taste*, Cambridge

Guyer, Paul, *Kant and the Claims of Knowledge*, Cambridge

Kant, I. *Metaphysical Foundations of Natural Science*, trans.
James Ellington, The Bobbs-Merrill Company, 1970

Kant, I., *Critique of Judgement*, trans J.C.Meredith, Oxford
University Press

Kant, I., *Critique of Practical Reason*, trans. T. Abbott, Longmans,
1909.

Kant, I., *Religion within the Bounds of Reason Alone*,
trans.T.Greene

and H. Hudson, Open Court 1960

Kant. I, *Critique of Pure Reason*, trans. N. Kemp-Smith,
    MacMillan, 1929

Kant, I., *Philosophical Correspondence*, ed. Arnulf Zweig,
    University of Chicago Press, 1967

Kant, I., *Prolegomena to any Future Metaphysics*, trans. P.Lucas,
    Manchester, 1978

Kant, I., *Groundwork of the Metaphysics of Morals*, trans. H.
    Paton, Hutchinson, 1956

Kant, I, *Metaphysics of Morals* (part II)), trans. J. Ellington, Bobbs
    Merrill, 1964

Kant, I., *Political Writings*, Cambridge, 1996

McCloskey, Mary, *Kant's Aesthetics*, State University of New
    York Press, 1987

Scruton, Roger, *Kant*, Oxford, 1982

Strawson, Sir Peter, *The Bounds of Sense*, Metheun 1966

Thomson, Garrett, *An Introduction To Modern Phlosophy*,
    Wadsworth Press, 1993

Walker, Ralph, *Kant*, Routledge, 1979

Walsh, W.H., *Kant's Criticisms of Metaphysics*, Edinburgh, 1975

K.Ward *The Development of Kant's Views on Ethics*, Basil
    Blackwell, 1972,

Wood, Allen, *Kant's Moral Religion*, Cornell, 1970

Wolff, Robert Paul, *The Autonomy of Reason*, Harper and Row,
    1973